On God's Flight

A Quest for the Breath of Life

Eutana Ree Herzig

Copyright   2017 Eutana Ree Herzig
SECOND EDITION
Edited by Martha Petrie Millard
Cover design by Parker Norman, Graphic and Interactive Media Designer,
pnorman.design@gmail.com

Dedication

To John, Katie, and Abbie you are precious; you are the air I breathe. To the extended family and friends that stood up, looked up, and locked their hearts and hands with John and me through this journey of faith.

To the One that my heavenly Father wants to reach with this message of my family's journey. May you find the Father's hand.

Table of Contents

PROLOGUE 5
CHAPTER ONE: The Passenger 21
CHAPTER TWO: Boarding the Flight 35
CHAPTER THREE: The Layover 47
CHAPTER FOUR: Flight Diverted 72
CHAPTER FIVE: The Takeoff 90
CHAPTER SIX: The Flight 123
CHAPTER SEVEN: The Arrival 175
EPILOGUE 209
GOD'S FINGERPRINT 221

PROLOGUE

We were about to the gate and my heart was racing. It was dark except for the lights lining the runway, but I could see the plane taxing up to the small arrival area of the airport. A long local county road off state Highway 412 led us to the entrance to Woodring Airport in Enid, Oklahoma. It was early April on the prairie and still cold on this Sunday night. It was a clear night, and we could see a light ten to fifteen miles away. We had to be at the airport promptly at 10:00 p.m. to meet the EagleMed flight from Wichita, Kansas, that would take John to Love Field in Dallas.

As we rounded the county road to the airport, we saw the midflight plane land and taxi up to the main terminal. The locked gate entering the airport stopped us. I glanced over at John, and he was wrapped in a blanket wearing his yellow Shidler Tiger's hoodie.

The heater was blasting and he was still cold. Near the gate, there was a box to place a code into, but no instructions on how to gain access to the code. There was no intercom either, so I rolled the truck window down to really look for a way to enter the gate. I got out of the pickup to look for a button next to the box and there wasn't anything. With no directions on how to get into the airport, I began to panic. I never thought to get the telephone number of the airport. How many people would think their local airstrip was locked up tighter than a jug?

"What can we do I asked John?" "You are not missing this flight."

Light emerged when I saw the plane door open up and could see medical personnel and a pilot exiting down the airplane steps. The airport terminal was dark as if no one was home. We were sitting approximately five hundred yards behind the gate from the terminal. Who's minding the airport? I thought. The tension and anxiety of waiting was getting the better of me, and I was now perspiring in forty-degree weather.

"Hold on I'm calling the police department," John said.

He got someone on the line and explained our circumstances and asked them to please hurry because the plane was waiting on the ground. We only had so long to get on the flight and get to Dallas as transplant protocol dictates. John had a three-hour window to get to the University of Texas Southwestern where Clements University Hospital was located, and where the lungs would be brought for transplantation. A medical team would retrieve the new lungs, and then the lungs would be transported to the hospital. The doctors would watch them and decide if they were viable.

John had to be there to begin a regiment of anti-rejection drugs prior to the surgery so time was precious. If we were late, the lungs could possibly go to another transplant candidate. It seemed like an old grandfather clock was ticking in my head, and it was becoming louder as the time went by waiting for a gate to open.

I told John, "I'll just take the gate with the truck if they don't give us a code to get in."

Me, Eutana Herzig, the pillar of following the rules, was now going to go up on federal charges for breaking into an airport. A five foot two Edward G was getting in there, see. I must be watching too much television to think of this 1930's gangster. I didn't care it was a choice between keeping John alive or smashing up a metal gate, so it wasn't a choice at all. John smiled hoping this would ease the rising tension, for he knew I was on the brink of angry.

My daughter, Abbie, and her roommate, Jordan, were behind us in her car. They were both going to make the trip to

Dallas. Earlier that evening the girls came home just expecting an ordinary Sunday dinner with their parents, but the call came right as the girls walked in the door. God's timing was always perfect. I called the girls and said we were trying to gain access, and if we didn't get in soon, I would ram the gate. I heard laughter from their car. Katie, my oldest daughter, and Harry, our grandson, decided to drive on to her apartment in Moore, Oklahoma, and I was to pick them up on my way through Oklahoma City.

Katie told her Dad goodbye in our bedroom. Katie and Abbie took a picture together with John and told their Daddy how much they loved him before we loaded him in the truck. Katie asked God to be with him during the surgery. She later told me that she wondered if that would be the last picture taken with her dad. You have to laugh to keep the emotions in check, but I was hell bent on getting my husband on this plane and on his way to Dallas. I was feeling the blood rise in my cheeks and angry was on the way when I thought, God is in charge, not these people who have the airport code. With that thought, I began to relax a bit and just bowed my head, closed my eyes, and took a deep breath. I could hear John breathing, the sound of the oxygen flowing through the tubes from the tank, and the deafening silence while we waited.

Finally, we heard the click; the gate began to open. The metal gate slid to the left and to the right, splitting in the center. After the heart-wrenching wait of ten minutes, I yelled out "Oh, my God!" I took in a deep breath and exhaled, put the truck in drive, and stepped on the gas. John's head swung back against the headrest as I gunned it through the gate. He glanced at me and knew he should not say anything, but cracked a smile. A road sign said ten miles per hour, but that seemed a little conservative being no traffic and all. My stomach lit up, queasy with excitement. All the pent up emotions and anxiety of just getting to the airplane caused my eyes to well up with tears. Thoughts of never seeing John again began to tug at my heart. The thought of what if I don't make it to Dallas in time kept running through my mind. My heart wrenched to think of all the devastating possibilities.

I pulled up to the parking area behind a chain link fence with a gate nearby. The plane was only twenty feet from the gate. John got out and waved at the pilot standing at the foot of the steps to the plane. My thoughts were beginning to stress me, and I bowed my head and asked God to take this from me. My God is my fortress and my strength, remembering that truth bumped into all those doubts and it snapped me back to the task at hand which was asking God to help. Just help me do this, God. I am so afraid so just hold my hand, God. I thank you for my husband, John, my beautiful daughters, and the donor who is giving John the gift of life. Please send your angels with him on this flight to Dallas, Texas. Amen.

    I slowly got out of the truck and wiped my tears on to the sleeve of my sweatshirt. As I approached, John was talking to the pilot. The pilot was in his mid-forties, and his name was Mr. Frey. John told him he would say goodbye to his wife, get his small bag, and then would be ready to board. John turned around and pulling his oxygen tank behind him went over to Abbie. John hugged her and told her how much he loved her. He also told her that God had this. I got his small bag and came back to the sidewalk. I heard John state that everything was going to be okay. Abbie has always kept things to herself and is a strong young woman, but I know there were tears as she walked back to her car. She then allowed John and me to have some time together alone before he boarded the plane.

Jordan, Abbie's roommate, took some pictures of the plane with her iPhone, and got back into the car. John and I just held each other for the longest time before we spoke.

"I want you to know life has been an adventure with you," I said. "You are the only man who has ever loved me. You're the smartest man I've ever known."

We both smiled at each other.

"I've been so blessed to be your wife for the last twenty-nine years, and I'm looking forward to our thirtieth anniversary, so promise me you'll be here".

He said, "I promise."

The things we should say, and the way we feel should be said more often. It shouldn't take a catastrophe to bring these up with the person you love. We were too busy with life's distractions that we didn't say the important things until we may not have had another chance to say them. Letting go of his hand, watching him walk towards the airplane gutted me. The tears rolled down my face. This moment took the breath from me. I knew I had to let him go.

I said to John, "Lance will be waiting for you at the hospital, and he will stay with you until I get there."

John began to cry, and his voice cracked as he told me how much he loved me and that God has this. He came back then hugged me once again and kept saying that he loved me. John and I clung to each other for the longest time and cried. This must be how all the soldiers and their wives must feel when going off to war. It ripped my heart out. It could be our last kiss, but I trusted that to Jesus.

I noticed his labored breathing and knew he needed to sit down, so I motioned for the medical team to come over and help him board the plane. Mr. Koehn and Mrs. Pata were registered nurses assigned to John's flight. They unhooked his oxygen line and handed it to me for they had all the necessary equipment on board. As John entered the plane, his large six foot nine inch frame filled the tiny jet door and blocked out most of the light. His presence dwarfed anyone near him both physically and in spirit. One nurse led him and the other followed behind him. Without the oxygen, he struggled for breath, especially when he was excited. When he got through the door he turned, waved, and blew me a kiss. I stood there on the tarmac for the longest time just watching until they closed the door.

My heart was broken, and I couldn't seem to let him go, not even in the hands of professionals. Life had forced me to relinquish control of the one person who was the most important to me in this world. It was despair. I was sick to my stomach. They had assured me he would be in good hands all the way to Dallas. I knew that already; he was in God's hands.

It wasn't long before the plane taxied out to the dark runway. I watched the plane until I couldn't see the flashing lights on its wings any longer. I was standing on the tarmac alone. It was unexplainable. One must experience it to know what it means. After John's departure, I headed back to the truck rolling the oxygen bottle behind me to begin the trip to Dallas. I kept thinking about John's calm demeanor, the look in his eyes when he said, "God's got this." I will see John again, and he will have new lungs.

Abbie hollered at me, "Let's go Momma".

I wiped the warm tears from my eyes and got into the truck. The highway south was barren on a late Sunday night. No, traffic just my daughter in her car behind me. It occurred to me that the steaks we were supposed to have for dinner would not keep until we returned. I hoped my mother would be all right by herself. Mother lived in a small house attached to ours. She no longer drove a car, so she would have to be brave until someone could come to the farm and pick her up tomorrow.

I was driving the truck alone, loaded with two oxygenators, twenty bottles of oxygen, and all our suitcases. My thoughts drifted in a hundred different directions with question after question. I began crying again. Every thought would make me tear up and get emotional. So, I began asking my heavenly Father some questions from the heart. *How did we get here, God? Life has been so smooth until now. Why is all this happening? Is there a purpose to this? Please tell me Lord, and I will do whatever it is you want us to do. He is only fifty-eight years old and has a lot of living left to do. Please God, help us through this. Show us what we are to know or learn.*

I finally stopped trying to bargain with the Great I Am and said aloud to myself, "He wants you to trust and obey, so stop these thoughts." I was reminded of the lesson of the withered fig tree. Jesus demonstrated his power and his faith to the disciples by cursing the barren fig tree and it withered away just as it was commanded to do. Jesus was showing the disciples they have this power also through their faith.

Jesus answered and said unto them, "Have faith in God. For assuredly I say to you, whoever says to the mountain, "Be removed and cast into the sea," and does not doubt in his heart, but believes that those things he says will be done, he will have whatever he says. Therefore, I say to you, whatever things you ask when you pray, believe that you receive them, and you will have them," (Mark 11:22-24) *KJV*.

I prayed, I believed, I drove, and I knew it would come to pass. The road stretched out before me, the hypnotic sound of the tires running over the asphalt calming me down. My mind jumped around when I drove. The pages of life blew backwards in my mind, and I thought, it was just the other day, when I first saw John.

CHAPTER ONE
"The Passenger"

I still see John as young and energetic. He was just a huge man, a blue-eyed, blond haired, big German specimen with an Okie twang. He was six foot nine, wore a fifteen shoe, and was my big teddy bear. He had a heart as big as his shoe size. Many people called him, Big John. Strangers always asked if he played basketball, and I always responded with, "No, he played miniature golf."

I noticed this guy while I was waiting for a job interview. It was the summer of 1982, and I had moved to Oklahoma City from Bartlesville, Oklahoma, where I had served for the past two years as a school counselor. There were three people sitting in a row outside the principal's office waiting to be interviewed for a teaching position at Del Crest Junior high School in Del City, Oklahoma. I looked down at the floor and then leaned over to the lady next to me and whispered, "Look at the size of the feet on that guy." She just raised her eyebrows and smiled. This huge man stood up and went in for his interview, and the next time I saw him was in the first faculty meeting that September when school began. I found out his name when the principal introduced the new faculty members. He was the woodshop teacher and would coach boys' basketball and track.

For the next five years, we rode the yellow dog together. Coaches referred to a school bus as a yellow dog. Seats were hard as hell, and they smelled like dirty kids or dogs, and they were yellow. We played ball for four and a half months every year with many out-of-town games. I taught seventh and eighth grade English and coached the ladies basketball teams. Both men and women's teams rode the same bus, so we became well acquainted.

To keep things interesting, John and I played many jokes on one another. This playful practice was contagious and the pranks on others were cramped. It kept us laughing and built cohesiveness among the faculty. I once sent a student down to John's shop to retrieve a left-handed hammer. A note was returned, sealed in an envelope. I could not share with anyone. The car door handles in the faculty parking lot mysteriously were greased with trombone slide grease and getting into the faculty members' cars was most difficult. We also hid the Spanish teacher's desk and numerous times staff members complained about their missing grade books.

Our Grammy Award winning moment came filling up the principal's office with balloons. When the principal opened his door, balloons rolled out of the room spilling into the main office. Students in the office kicked them out into the main hall and kids began to play ball and pop them. Needless to say it caused a lot of chaos. There was hell to pay, but no one confessed to the crime, so the whole faculty was admonished. The janitors were unhappy; they were the ones who had to get rid of the balloons. The students were thrilled by all the balloons and thought it was funny.

There were twelve single teachers on a faculty of forty-five. The dirty dozen always did things together. We planned skiing trips, went to Europe in the summer, and always went for drinks on the Friday of payday. I remember fixing John up with every girl friend or old sorority sister that lived in Oklahoma City area, but nothing stuck. He was high maintenance and still immature in some ways. Just mature enough to hold down a professional job, but still ready to party. I was like a big sister, six years older than John, with no intentions of becoming romantically entangled. I had purchased a condo, a house full of new furniture, and drove a black limited edition MGB convertible. I was in tall cotton, so to speak.

He finally asked me out to dinner four years later. I had returned from a three-month tour of Europe and brought him a crucifix blessed by the Pope. I had been gone all summer and missed my friend, and I believe he missed me too. We went to dinner that very night, had too much to drink, and that was the end of a beautiful friendship and the beginning of a thirty-year stroll together. He introduced me to his parents and family that very Thanksgiving holiday; I guess you might say it stuck. He was my best male friend, and we knew almost everything about each other. No one at school had a clue about our relationship. We had been thrown together as coaches and were always together. We wrote notes to each other and placed them in our faculty mailboxes. We quietly had a courtship behind the scenes. Our new names became Margaret and Frank. *M.A.S.H.* was a popular television show we watched each night and that was where we stole our new identities. It was all fun and romantic until one day I realized I loved John. That scared me. Someone may get hurt, and it may be me. We took a mutually agreed dating sabbatical. We were both miserable at least I was for the next three months. That spring was hard because we were track coaches and had to be around each other so much of the time.

In April a dozen red roses were delivered to the school office with a sealed card attached. Someone called my room on the intercom and told me that I had something that had just been delivered to me. Eyebrows were raised when they saw it was for Miss Tana Rigsby. The secretaries and the office aids watched as I read the card. I could not hold it back, and I smiled as I bent over and smelled the roses and then returned to class. That very night in John's bachelor pad on Walker Street, John got down on one knee and proposed to me. A month later in the last faculty meeting of the school year, we announced we were getting married. You could have heard a pin drop and everyone drew in a big breath. When the shock was over, they rather liked the idea. All of a sudden, the faculty began to clap and cheer. You might say our relationship started with a love of the game of basketball and ended in a love for each other.

The wedding was on for August, so we had a short time to plan a small event. Many showers and parties through the month of June, but on the Fourth of July all hell broke loose, and John called the wedding off. A case of cold feet was the expression people used to describe the unfortunate situation. I was devastated and retreated from everyone for weeks. John called and wanted to see the priest together in late July. After several counseling sessions with the priest, the wedding was back on for later in August. With most of the faculty present, we said our nuptials. I knew the priest had his doubts about the longevity of the marriage, because he said so during the ceremony. I will never forget it. The priest was talking about us as a couple and each couple has some difficulties in their relationships that they must work out. This couple is older and set in their ways the priest said and I'm not sure they wanted give up their current life style. All of sudden Father said, "Are they going to make it?" "I don't know, but God knows". Our friends and guests that filled the pews burst into laughter. Father Donaho was an Irishman with a terrific sense of humor and a quaint Irish accent. He was a darling to me and helped us through a difficult time.

      The school year flew by and in June, my doctor told me I was expecting a baby.

John was elated about the news and couldn't wait to tell his parents. Soon all of our family and the school family knew that Mr. and Mrs. Herzig were going to have a new addition. Junior high kids thought it was cool that the coaches were having a baby. John was very protective and screened out some activities he thought might be too taxing for his pregnant wife. He was having pains right along with me and shared that he hoped he would not freeze to death before the baby arrived. The students also expressed a concern for they wore their coats to English class when they saw Mrs. Herzig had the windows open. It was a long winter for all those around this expectant mother who did not need a coat of any kind. Katie Rose Herzig arrived four minutes after midnight on March 1, 1988, just short of being born on the twenty-ninth day of February of a leap year.

As an old married couple, we stayed at Del Crest for one more year and then fled to the rural life to raise our daughter. John said he had to take a job as an education administrator in Wilburton, Oklahoma, to start out in order to move upward in his career.

"Okay," I said, "where is this town?"

"The Kiamichi Mountains located in southeast Oklahoma!" John said.

Yes, I did roll my eyes. We moved to the sticks. This was a three-hour drive southeast of Oklahoma City. John was going to be the middle school principal, and I wound up getting a job as the high school counselor. It was a cozy little town, over the mountain, east of the only city for hundreds of miles. John introduced me to Buddy Ennis, superintendent for Wilburton Public Schools. He was vertically challenged when standing next to John. He hired me in his office that day and gave us some helpful information concerning the locals. Mr. Ennis warned us not to drive in any direction into the forest. Of course, I asked him, "Why?"

"People in the hills have illegal activity and even the federal officials enter armed and with caution."

"In other words we could be shot, right?"

"Yes," he said smiling and walked away.

With that bit of information, we concluded that there would be no Sunday driving to see the countryside. Wilburton had only one stop light, and they turned it off at seven o'clock in the evening. No doubt, we found ways to pass the time. John and I always talked about having normal sized children. We were an unusual pair for I stood five foot two in my favorite pumps. My standing next to John would make anyone grin. Our children are tall, blond, blue-eyed and have no Native American traits from their mother. Cherokee women are generally short, rounded faces with high cheekbones, dark hair, and golden toned skin. I can trace our lineage back to northeastern Georgia before the trail of tears. Adair County in Oklahoma was named after a relative. My name is Cherokee and was given to me by my Grandfather Adair. There was no visual evidence that I had anything to do with bringing them into this world, except the extraordinary character and poise both my children possess. While still in Wilburton, Oklahoma, our second daughter, Abbie, arrived on June 20, 1991.

Two years rolled by and John had to move each time to move up in the field of education. John served two years as high school principal in Wewoka, Oklahoma. The superintendent at Wewoka was an old FBI agent named Bill, and when he hired John, he knew more about John than John knew about himself. It was here that Katie began kindergarten. Her first teacher just happened to be Judy. This was Superintendent Bill's wife. Katie had a wonderful first school experience there and we are all still friends to this day. Abbie was a two-year-old toddler and got into everything. We played a lot of golf and lived there two years before we moved to give John a chance at becoming a superintendent.

It was on to Drummond, Oklahoma, where he served as superintendent of schools. This little town was very close to Enid. I became the high school counselor at Pioneer High School, a small rural school fifteen miles from Drummond and in the middle of the prairie.

Two years later John came home, and said he was going to leave education. I thought he had lost his marbles, but John left the field of education for a business realm. We owned Herzig's Digicopy Incorporated, an Authorized Xerox Sales Agency. We moved to Ada, Oklahoma, for the next two years and opened a store.

We moved for the last time when the Xerox headquarters sent him back to Enid, Oklahoma, to open a store. John and I ran the business until 2008 when we came full circle and reentered education. I began working in the seventh school district of my career before retiring six years later from Chisholm Public Schools while John was employed at Shidler, Oklahoma, as superintendent. Shidler is an hour and forty minutes from our home in Enid, so during the school year he lived in a house provided by the school district. On the weekends, he would come home unless he needed to stay for games and tournaments. Living and working in Shidler continued for seven years.

CHAPTER TWO
"Boarding the Flight"

In May 2015, John came home for the weekend from Shidler. Seven long years of seeing him only on the weekends had passed. We made the most of the time we had together whether in work or play. At this time, our girls were in college and high school, so I stayed in Enid working and taking care of our family farm. Home was eighty acres of grassland with a few trees and a pond we dug for the dozen head of cattle we owned. We raised and ate our own beef. There was work to do each weekend, and John and I did our best to fix up the old house and keep life nailed together. A bountiful garden bloomed each spring. We both loved the peace and quiet found only in the country. It was a wonderful place for the tribe to gather on holidays. My side of the family was always referred to as the tribe because of our Native American heritage.

The month of May signaled the end of the school year, and the end of John's seventh year as superintendent of Shidler Public Schools. We'd been getting some errands done and pulled into the drive to unload our haul from town. I was carrying in some bags, and as I went back out the door, I saw John resting on the pickup with his groceries, trying to catch his breath. He took in deep breaths but was gasping for more air. He was shaking and almost panicked for lack of air. He hadn't walked five feet from the back of the pickup.

"What's wrong with you?" I asked.

"I've been having a very hard time breathing lately," he growled back.

"Get ready," I said, "because I'm making you a doctor's appointment to see what's going on."

He complained he couldn't take the time off work. I told him nothing at school was more important than his health. At the appointment with the pulmonologist, it was as if God's flight attendant had placed a hand to his mouth and shouted "All aboard." We boarded God's flight that very day which took us on His journey.

The month of June flew by, and Dr. Whitson, the pulmonologist, in Enid scheduled tests in the hospital after the Fourth of July holiday. The family tribe had a big party planned for the fourth at our farm. The tribe showed up for a two-day stay to hoot, holler, and pop a firecracker or two. We played volleyball, horseshoes, and cards, and the little kids swam in the new horse tank. The old timers relaxed on the screened-in-porch. The smoker was at work cooking ribs and brisket, which permeated the air. We had our annual water gun fight and all were soaked before the completion of the activity.

Participation by all was required and was enforced. It was hot and all enjoyed getting wet. This was a sobering event. We formed the family circle holding hands and a word of prayer was said before the meal was served. Naps ensued before the fireworks show that started at dusk. With thirty members or more, we had plenty of fireworks to let off. Our farm was decorated with numerous flags for the annual fireworks show and was accompanied by the patriotic songs of John Phillip Sousa blaring from the porch. You heard the oohs and awes from the crowd lined up in their lawn chairs in front of the red milking barn. Following the show, the little ones were off to bed, and then the big poker game on the porch. Many lost their pot of gold at the tribal table and one lucky person had the bragging rights until next year. Family time this year was precious.

John checked into Integris Bass Hospital in Enid early on Monday morning after the holiday. Dr. Whitson had a lung biopsy and some heart tests scheduled that very day. He had a private room, and he had to get a bed extension, as John's legs were too long for a regular hospital bed. Dr. Whitson explained the procedure he was about to perform. He was a no-nonsense fellow and got right to the point. He would go down into the lungs, take a small piece of tissue, and have it sent to the lab. Dr. Schrader, a heart specialist, said he would do his procedure first and see what, if anything, was going on with his heart. They suspected hypertension because of the labored breathing. This was an enlargement of the heart on one side.

John was gone all afternoon, and I waited in his room reading and snoozing. Finally, he was rolled back into the room with drain tubes placed in his chest. He was sleeping, and the nurse said it would be awhile before the doctor would come and talk to us. When the doctor did arrive, he had x-rays in his hand to show us something. He wanted us to see the gaping black areas in John's lungs. John's lung function was less than twenty percent in the left lung and less than fifty percent in the right lung. He didn't have the function of one whole lung with the two of them working together. He told us the pathology report would be back in a few days to determine a diagnosis, and that the tubes would have to be out of his lungs for twenty-four hours before he could return home. The lungs had to seal and heal properly where the tubes had been inserted. This went well, and we went home on the fourth day in the hospital with orders to see Dr. Whitson the next day in his office.

    We were home about twenty four hours when John collapsed outside. He was bent over holding on to an electric pole outside our house. I backed the pickup up to where he was standing and helped him into the cab of the truck.

"Don't fall, honey, I will not be able to pick you up!" I shouted.

He was wheezing and gasping for air, and I thought he was going to pass out before I could get him into the truck. I knew I could get him to the hospital faster than calling an ambulance, so I sped through all the traffic lights with my caution lights flashing. The emergency room team took him away on a gurney as I took in a deep breath and drove to the ER parking lot. I rushed back into the hospital, and sure enough, my instincts were right, his left lung had collapsed. The doctors kept him another six days. While he was there the pathologist's report came back: idiopathic pulmonary fibrosis. To be sure, Dr. Whitson sent his information to Michigan Medical Consultants to confirm the diagnosis.

The doctor said John's condition was serious, yet John and I didn't understand how serious. Maybe we were in denial about his diagnosis. The internet gave us enough information to scare us. I kept thinking it wasn't that bad. John had huge black holes in his lungs where normal tissue was replaced with fibrous tissue. He also had pulmonary hypertension, which caused the right side of his heart to work harder and become enlarged because his lungs were deficient. We came back to see Dr. Whitson in his office for John's post hospital appointment. The doctor finished his examination, and that was when it happened. John asked the big question.

"How serious is this condition, doctor?" "From what I've read on the internet it's a death sentence."

The doctor took a moment before he replied.

"You should get your affairs in order," the doctor calmly replied. "Apply for disability, and call for an appointment at the Nazih Zudi Transplant Institute in Oklahoma City, and I will call and send them your records."

John said, "I need to retire then?"

"You will become weaker and have lots of appointments with doctors. You will have to make the retirement decision, but it may take some time to get disability," the doctor said.

John was put on two liters of continuous oxygen to sustain him and give him adequate oxygen to perform his daily functions. He ran an entire school system with personnel, plant management duties, and financial oversight of the school district. He had to make numerous decisions and needed to feel better and think clearly, but the sum of all fears was just thrust upon us. I sat there with this blank stare on my face. John was processing this news as well, and then he looked over to me with this empty look in his eyes. The thought John is going to die ran through my head. The doctor's voice had receded into a tunnel and was barely audible as he matter-of-factly delivered the news that

John was going to die if he didn't get a transplant. I felt like someone took their hand, reached into my chest, and ripped out my heart. I was suddenly nauseous and felt my face flush.

I looked over at John just sitting there and could tell he was in shock. So was I. Neither of us shed a tear until we got home. My mind raced. How do you face death when it comes slowly stealing your breath and forcing you to dwell on it day after day? I'd rather be plowed over with a semi-truck and go in an instant. I don't know what was going through John's mind, but mine had rocketed into panic mode. I always carried my Bible around in my arms when I was going through a valley. Let me tell you, we had fallen into Grand Canyon. I grasped for all God's words I had stored in my memory. I whispered to myself, "He will never leave you nor forsake you." (Hebrews 13:5) *KJV* and many other verses to find strength to face what had just become our reality.

"Be still, and know that I am God," (Psalm 46:10) *KJV* helped stop the mental horror of losing the man I loved for so many years. *How could I live on without him?* I just didn't want to. I had to stop this type of destructive thinking, so I muttered prayers all day no matter what task I was doing. I wasn't going to let Satan into my thoughts any longer. I wiped the tears away and from that point on, I cried out of John's sight. I was the new attitude in town and put on the whole armor of God! John and I spent twenty-nine years together. We both knew God had a plan, so we started doing exactly what the doctor requested.

How did one get one's affairs in order? We at least had to make a list, and we started making appointments with the lawyer, the teacher's retirement system, the social security administration, and the undertaker.

With all this to do, John returned to work for the school year which was about to start in August. He wanted to keep the diagnosis under wraps until he knew when he could retire. I sarcastically thought. I'll be here, honey, waiting and worrying for the both of us. So, I waved and blew him a kiss as he headed down the driveway returning to Shidler for another school year. The tears slid down my face as I realized he would be back home to stay sooner than he thought. Our appointment at the Nazih Zuhdi Transplant Institute in Oklahoma City was only three weeks away.

I heard one of God's angels come on the loud speaker and say, "Please buckle your seat belts and place all carryon luggage in the overhead compartment for we will be taking off momentarily. Fear of the unknown and what we would encounter on this flight engulfed me as I desperately clung to my Bible and constantly conversed with God.

CHAPTER THREE
"The Layover"

At our first appointment at the Nazih Zuhdi Transplant Institute, our expectations were that it would be a short visit with no more than an hour with the doctor; we would be home for Labor Day weekend. Well, one hour turned into four amazing and emotional hours. We spent time with the transplant coordinator, Brianna Wallace. She was an optimistic sunny personality that checked John's vitals and typed his medical history as she spoke to him. She spoke of the required six-minute walks, as well as, spirometry tests at each appointment. The spirometry measured John's lung function, which was vital to evaluating his digression of the disease.

Dr. Qasim Mirza, was soft spoken with an eastern accent, told us that John could feel fine one day and fall gravely ill the next with this disease. The doctor said John had to be nicotine free for six months before they would consider placing him on the transplant list. John had dipped tobacco for some time after he quit smoking years ago.

"I'm willing to do that no problem," John said.

He took the Skoal can out of his pocket and threw it in the trashcan in front of the doctor.

"Okay," the doctor said. "We will test your blood each visit to confirm you are nicotine free. You will maintain a healthy weight level and pass a six-minute walk at every monthly scheduled appointment."

John had a few extra pounds to lose but was close to the required BMI range for transplantation. Next, the social worker, Robert Cross came in the examining room.

He was an older, grey haired man that asked John some mental health questions. He talked about the emotional roller coaster that patients sometimes felt they were on. He gave us information and brochures about some support groups that met here at this hospital that we could join. Many waiting organ recipients and some already on the waiting list participated in the groups. He told us that depression, which sometimes could occur, had a detrimental effect on your physical health as well. This session was the shortest of all the sessions. He should have asked me some questions because I was on the brink of a meltdown. I guessed spouses were not the main focus.

    The financial coordinator, Jennifer Peet, entered the room and asked us to move to a conference room. We were glad to stand up for we were almost three hours into this visit. She had her arms full of materials and put it them on the table. She inundated us with so much information including fund raising, costs of the transplant, and financial issues that we had to ask for a few moments to get our composure. She left a box of tissues on the table and said she would give us some time. I broke down; John and I both cried like babies. Watching a six-foot man cry wasn't easy, but this was my sweetheart. I was consumed with a type of grief similar to a death occurring. Weeping wasn't sufficient enough of a word to describe our condition. We saw the mountain we each had to climb and didn't know if we could do it. Alternatively, we considered if living, I mean really living during the time that the doctors said John had left on this earth, might be a better option. Maybe two years was our understanding from Dr. Whitson when we first knew about this condition. I knew right then God had to be consulted.

    I asked God: *take this decision from us, and we would do His will and not ours.*

Paul said, "to be anxious for nothing, but in everything by prayer and supplication, with thanksgiving, let your requests be known to God; and the peace which surpasses all understanding will guard you hearts and minds through Jesus Christ." (Philippians 4:6) *KJV*. Neither of us realized how many challenges lie ahead of us, but I knew who was piloting our plane. And with that knowledge, I clung to this verse for peace during all the turbulence.

The doctor said it would be six months getting on a transplant list. *Jesus could return by the time he could get on a list,* I happily thought. I quickly went through six months in my head. It was March 2016, a long time from today.

John would come home and get unstressed to stay healthy enough for a transplant. In the meantime, he had many tests at the Integris Bass Hospital in Oklahoma City to complete: a CT scan, aortic ultrasound, colonoscopy, carotid ultrasound, esophagram, ventilation/perfusion scan, ECHO, EKG, spirometry, pulmonary function test, and many others. Each monthly doctor visit, John took his six-minute walk and weighed in to verify he was watching his weight. The doctor kept reiterating the need to maintain his health. He said some patients became so ill they would be placed on a ventilator while waiting for a transplant. John spoke very clearly and loudly to the doctor; he was not waiting on a ventilator. He absolutely said he would not lie in a hospital bed and wait to get a transplant, and I had to promise not to allow this to happen. He stated that plainly in his Power of Attorney documents.

"It is a race for time," the doctor said. "This program only considers patients that are healthy enough for a transplant, therefore, staying as healthy as you possibly can enhance the possibility you will get a spot on the transplant list." A panel of medical personnel consisting of doctors, surgeons, social workers, and nurses voted on the candidates, but we were a long way from that particular part of the process. They gave us a list of tests John had to undergo before they would consider him for a transplant. John had already done some of these in Enid, so he was left with around fifteen to do at the hospital in Oklahoma City. He had to see a dentist and a dermatologist and we made those appointments with our doctors in between their appointment times in Oklahoma City. The weekend gave us time to talk, but mostly we cried and John became angry, as well.

"I don't know if I'm going to do this," he said abruptly. "I'm not putting my family through the financial burden this will entail. We worked hard all these years for this little farm, and I'm not leaving you and the kids with nothing."

"So this is all about money, right? This is not about time with your family," I said.

He exploded. I couldn't let him imply that money was so important to his family when he knew damn well it wasn't. I grew up poor as a church mouse. I had a meal and a warm place to sleep. My parents did not attend or finish college. Our family was dysfunctional to say the least, so I worked my way through college and then a master's degree to dig myself out of the ghetto so to speak. I could go back to work, but I couldn't stand the thought of John refusing to try. I became so upset; I was physically ill. I felt like my ulcer was back.

I got my Bible, carried it around and talked to the Lord, who always had the answer, for he knew our outcome already. Faith, faith was what was so hard for us at times. While we tried so hard to rest in His arms, we made the human error of taking matters into our own hands. "Blessed is the man who makes the Lord his trust." (Psalm 40:4) *KJV*. I struggled with this all of my life. Trust was hard for me. There were not a lot of people I trusted growing up. I thought if you did it yourself, you were not disappointed, and this became a life-long conviction.

Three kinds of faith exist: the struggling believer who flounders in open water, the clinging believer who clings to God's boat, and the resting believer who sits quietly resting in God's boat. We all strive to be the resting believers in God's boat, but human we are. Oh, how I prayed for strength each day to trust and obey. I believe that prayer opens the doors of heaven; therefore, my prayers released God's power on our present dilemma. I could not share our news with anyone, so I harbored this all in my heart and talked only to God until John made his decision. I prayed it would be soon so I could pray with my sisters and my friends. We are to share one another's burdens is what our Father says. Life's loads are not so heavy when someone else is there with you. I needed my family and friends.

At the last session with the financial coordinator, she told us that John had excellent insurance. As John was talking, I kept repeating to myself, we have excellent insurance. She handed us a break down of the transplant costs. The tests preceding surgery could be upwards of thirty thousand dollars. The operation could cost nearly three hundred fifty thousand dollars and the post-transplant drugs eleven thousand dollars a month for life. To a teacher, this was laughable. We had been in the public service industry and that kind of money we had never seen nor will we ever see it. I kept repeating we had excellent insurance. I even cracked a smile. I couldn't even say, *well, you can't take it with ya!* You had to have money before you say something so profound. I was counting on what the financial coordinator told us because she had seen what most insurance companies covered and did not. Fundraisers were too time consuming and would not raise enough money. Maybe if we had time for a thousand pancake suppers, still we might not have raised enough money. We didn't have time for that, we were in the fight and focused on finishing medical tests. My reaction to all of this was, "Duh," which was an indication of extreme stress.

The burden of telling our daughters was heavy. We had to, and we knew it had to be soon. The Adair Family Reunion was in one week on September 11, 2015. Everyone would see John's condition, so John and I had to agree on what to say to the family, until we told our daughters. So, we postponed telling the girls. As had been proven down through the years, if one tribal member knows something, before the setting sun all shall know the news. News was the only thing that doesn't run on Indian time, but was as swift as the dashing deer in the month of November. The Adair family are registered tribal members of the Cherokee Nation, and are a very tight knit bunch. I have three sisters with three or more children each, and Katie and Abbie were very close to their cousins. Love to all, fight with all, and forgiveness for all. We lived out our days as the Adair Family motto states: Loyalty to the death.

I had a dream in early March of 2015, about souls that were saved at the reunion, and called my nephew, Lance, that very morning. I never remembered my dreams but when I did, usually, God was trying to tell me something.

"Get ready," I said, "there is something big that God has on the agenda for the reunion this year."

Lance Hyde was my oldest nephew and a dynamic, Christian man. For some time, Lance had married and baptized members of the clan. John and Lance have had a lot of discussions about grace and works down through the years. Each conversation always ended in an agreement to disagree. The reunion week was upon us. It was time to head to Lake Murray in southern Oklahoma. The family had used this state facility many times. Lake Murray was just south of Ardmore, Oklahoma, nestled in the thick woods and this state lodge was perfect for family reunions. They had plenty of cabins if you reserved them in advance.

    My sister, Leesa, would be sharing an extra-large cabin that slept six. This cabin had a full cooking stove and refrigerator so the bulk of the food came over to us. I brought my turkey roaster and cooked pulled pork for Saturday's special feast. Sandwiches, chips, and drinks for about forty people was on the menu. Everyone brought desserts and some kind of side dish for that night. You were on your own the rest of the time. We played cards, hiked in the woods, or swam in the lake. There were plenty of activities to keep the family busy. We tried to have a campfire that all could gather around if it wasn't too warm.

We decided to wait and tell the girls about John's condition until after the reunion. We did not want to spoil this weekend. The laughter was good for my spirit. John enjoyed talking and seeing everyone. He explained that the doctor had put him on some oxygen because he had been short of breath and were going to run some additional tests this month. We played the delay game until we told the girls first.

On Sunday morning, the entire clan met at the lodge for breakfast. The waitresses there were so patient when forty people all at once invaded the dining room. This was a two-hour pancake fest, and you couldn't hear yourself think. Just keeping up with the tickets and what table they were sitting at was a nightmare. The goodbyes were a parade of hugs, and I'll write or call soon. This year we had one person who asked Lance to baptize them. Wouldn't you know it? Katie, my oldest daughter was going to be baptized. My dream had come true and this was big for me. The lake had red algae in it this year, and we were advised not to get into the water. The swimming pool was still available so that was where we were to meet for the baptism. We all sat poolside, and Lance and Katie entered the water. Kids splashed and yelled in the background, but this was a blessing no matter where we were.

Lance asked Katie, "Who is Jesus to you?"

"He's my Lord and savior," she told him without hesitation.

"This is your first act of obedience," Lance said. "Jesus said, if you profess me before men, I will profess you before my Father."

She went down into the water and was raised in the newness of Christ Jesus. She was to walk and become a new creature. She was made new and whole and will inherit eternal life. Everyone clapped, and I cried.

Lance asked, "Is there anyone else?"

He waited ever so long before starting for the swimming pool ladder, and then three others rose to their feet and started for the ladder. Abbie and two others were headed for the ladder. My heart pounded in my chest, I turned to look at my sisters in shock. I had been given a double blessing from my Lord. Tears rolled down my face as I stared up at the heavens to praise Him. Lance finished baptizing Abbie, Hope, and Dane.

"Lance said, "Is there anyone else? I'm already wet. Is there anyone?"

All of a sudden, my John rose from his chair and took the oxygen hose from his face. Everyone became quiet. My mouth was wide open. I was frozen, staring into his eyes as he moved closer to the pool. John proceeded to the ladder and began to take the steps carefully. He was shaking and sobbing. I stood and took his arm to steady him as he descended down the steps of the ladder. Lance was there and had a hold of him by the arms. As he reached the bottom of the stairs, Lance hugged him and held him for a long while. John's breathing was labored without the oxygen and it was evident as he turned and faced the family. John made Lance look small, and Lance was six foot or better in height. I was in tears. I had never thought this was the person in my dream.

Leesa, my sister, said; "Now this is big! We will be together for eternity."

I was crying and couldn't believe what was happening to my entire family.

"I don't know why, but all I can do lately is cry," John said to Lance.

Lance replied, "When you come to the end of yourself, God will take over."

I prayed that the Holy Spirit would comfort my loving husband, and John could feel his presence from this day forward. The family witnessing this did not know the challenges that lay ahead for John and our family. God knew. I was numb. We got John out of the water and dried him off and back on his oxygen. John had been forever changed. My entire family had been. My dream had come to fruition, and many souls were saved this year at the reunion. John had put on the whole armor of God for the battle that would take place in the next few weeks, months, or even years that required supernatural power and strength.

This verse I took to heart when Paul wrote: "Put on the whole armor of God, that you may be able to stand against the wiles of the devil…Stand therefore, having girded your waist with truth, having put on the breastplate of righteousness, and having shod your feet with preparation of the gospel of peace, above all, taking the shield of faith, wherewith ye shall be able to quench all the fiery darts of the wicked." (Ephesians 6:10-20) *KJV*. When things seemed to get dark or impossible, faith carried us through it. I began to realize that faith was the one thing I could cling to because I was not in control of anything-regarding John's condition or even his demise. I was his number one, my job was to love him and keep him organized as to his appointments and medical tests in the months to come.

John was still wrestling with the decision to move forward with getting on a transplant list or not. He would have audible arguments with himself as to having a transplant. I didn't think he realized that it had a devastating effect on me. I wanted him to live not fold. I took it all to heart, but was careful to suppress it. If any despair slipped out of me, John was down on himself and angered again about the situation once again.

I wanted to help him, but God was the only one who could tackle this task. I encouraged him to read his Bible.

"Honey, one day you will just know what the right thing is for you to do," I said softly. "He will deliver a veil of peace over you, and then you will have the answer. Look and you will find it in His Word," I encouraged John.

"I love you," he said.

We called our kids home for the weekend. We lied and told them we needed their help on the farm, which in reality wasn't such a lie. Dad was too weak and needed them I said, and I promised them I would fix a big steak for them on the grill if they would stay for dinner. It was time to tell them the whole truth about their Daddy. Telling the kids was far more emotional than we thought it would be. It was a crying session. It was a yelling session. I think Katie stomped her feet in anger. Katie was so much like her father that it was uncanny. She throws hissy fits, just like John. She is short tempered, outgoing, needy at times, a social butterfly, and just a beautiful person. She rushes into things, and she also learns things the hard way. Abbie has a lot of my temperament. She is stubborn and independent. Her artistic ability is phenomenal. If it were developed, she would be dangerous in the art world. She is humorous, and doesn't listen to others, but figures it out on her own. She hates drama. Abbie is tough as a boot and her Daddy's joy, but is a marshmallow inside. She has no concept of time and is a typical baby of the family.

We gathered in the big family room and the girls kept asking us what's this all about? We sat down and John looked over at me and then at the girls.

"I have a terminal disease called idiopathic pulmonary fibrosis," John quietly told them. "I haven't quite decided if I'm going to pursue a transplant."

The girls began to cry as he was telling them that he was weighing it out. For now, he would proceed as if he was going to try to get on the transplant list. They didn't agree with the idea of not trying. They became angry with John for considering any possibility of letting nature take its course. I was right there with them and joined in the fight. Yes, we ganged up on a man who was terminal.

"What about Harry, he needs his grandfather," Katie shouted.

"You're not a quitter, Dad," Abbie said sarcastically.

They used every guilt-ridden argument they could to get their dad to agree with them. The tears came soon after the anger. Their fear was a result of knowing the reality of the situation, and bad words to flew about the room during our family meeting. I had had time to let this news sink in, but they were going through all these emotions during the discussion. We were all drained emotionally and just sat in silence for a while. They were so torn up about the possibility of losing their dad. The girls sat and wept.

"I will proceed with the medical tests, and just see if I can get on a list," John said breaking the silence.

They both got up and hugged their Daddy and then hugged their mom satisfied that he was going to fight. We didn't even mention all the obstacles we would have to go around to get on a list. and that time was not on our side. Less than two years had been Dr. Whitson's prognosis. We withheld the fact that if John was to get on a list some people didn't get lungs in time and died. According to the current transplant statistics there were two thousand people waiting for a lung transplant nationwide and two hundred or more died waiting every year. The lungs are the most difficult organs to harvest because after death the donor's body is flooded with fluids that are harmful to the lungs in order to harvest the other organs such as the heart, kidneys, or liver. So many things could go wrong in the next six months, but John said he would try. Simply put if John failed one of the twenty-five or thirty tests, he would be without any chance of getting on a list.

The following weekend John asked his brother and sister to meet so he could share the news about his diagnosis. John had three siblings an older brother and two older sisters. On Sunday afternoon, we all gathered at Barbara's house in Enid. Sitting at Barbara's kitchen table John shared the news with Jim and Barb. Jane Ellen, the eldest, lived so far away that she was told the news by phone. They listened quietly and offered their support. John became emotional and had to stop to gain his composure. His brother and sister simply told him they would support his decision and would be there for him. John broke into tears again and told them he hadn't made the final decision to pursue a transplant. They all agreed to withhold this news from their elderly mother until a later date because of her numerous health concerns and how she might react.

CHAPTER FOUR
"Flight Diverted"

It was mid-October almost fall break and there were several appointments scheduled when John came back from school. He sounded very spent and tired over the phone. John arrived home and put his back pack down that holds his small oxygen tank.

"I can't work much longer. I can't even think straight some days and I don't have the stamina for all the baseball and softball games I should attend. We will have to borrow the money and buy out the rest of the time on my retirement. I have ninety days of sick leave left and that will take us through December, and I could officially retire." John said.

"Okay, when will you start taking the sick leave?" I asked.

"Soon after fall break," John replied.

He finally said it; he had to come home and rest. I could tell it was getting harder for him to breathe even with the oxygen. His October appointment was coming up. He called in sick and stayed an extended time at home. I could tell things were getting worse by the day. He struggled to do the little things. He didn't sleep well and struggled for air. I was losing sleep as well, just listening to him breath in rasps every night. I nudged him several times a night to make sure he was breathing. I had nightmares of him dying in his sleep, and I would wake up next to him. I was horrified and sleep depraved.

The doctor raised his oxygen level at the next appointment. They changed to a larger oxygen tank that could be pulled behind him. This would hold three times as much as the small tank. He performed a little worse on the required six-minute walk. John had several tests throughout October at the hospital and passed each one. In the meantime, John worked out his retirement. We made a trip to the teacher's retirement office at the state capitol and signed some papers, which finalized it.

When he returned to work after fall break, he took his ninety days of sick leave a week later and told everyone on the staff and the school board that he was terminally ill. I cringed each time I heard John use the word terminal, and telling others he was trying to get on a transplant list. When the news began to spread, the prayers could be felt. John spent a lot of time on the phone helping the new interim superintendent at the school. There were a lot of loose ends he had to attend to, and it was stressful for John. He loved that school district and the people there. We drove to Shidler, which was an hour and forty-five minutes from our farm, and packed up his house. About half of the baseball team showed up to help us load the trailer. The next stop was his office. This was hard for him. Eight years of his life had been spent in this office. We carried out two boxes of personal things. I knew how he felt and I kept silent. He was finished with his career in education for good.

The medical tests were ongoing. The list became longer not shorter it seemed. It was November now. We made many trips to Oklahoma City. He failed his last colonoscopy and was so angry. The prep for one of these was two days without food and some awful stuff you have to drink. The big thing was staying close to a restroom. If you followed the instructions, you became clean inside and out. John's mood I would describe as dark at the very least. This was his second go-round for this test. The doctor came into the recovery and began talking to John bedside.

"Careful I wouldn't get too close," I warned.

"Why?" the doctor asked.

"I'm afraid John will lash out at you if he's the least bit sedated."

The doctor took a step back and explained to both of us that he had another procedure he could try, and we would not have another colonoscopy. The doctor just saved his own life with the announcement of another procedure to try; John was not going to do this again.

It was now close to Thanksgiving and the doctor upped his oxygen again to five liters. A meeting was scheduled for the following month with the surgeon to find out what his recommendation was for John. Dr. Mirza said both lungs needed to be replaced, so we would see what the surgeon recommended. The consultation with this doctor was less than ten minutes. He told us one lung because he felt someone else could be saved sharing with two transplant patients. He was unemotional and short. We thanked him and left. We began to think they would not do a double or bilateral because of the risks involved. We didn't understand why these doctors could not agree. This went on and on. Finally, Dr. Mirza asked our permission to contact a doctor in Texas for his opinion. We agreed, of course, we wanted a second opinion.

The month of December, we took care of the lawyer and put all we had into a family trust. We had to do was locate every title to vehicles, tractors, trailers, farm equipment, locate property deeds, bank accounts, and list anything of value in the safe. All we had together would fit into a shoebox. This was extremely easy for we had a great friend, David Ezzell, who had helped us down through the years. As lawyers go, he was tops. That allowed us to check off one more task on our list.

The social security administration was a waiting game. The paper work was complete. We heard back from them before Christmas. He was cleared to collect his benefits. I guessed the government heard his diagnosis and received the letter from Dr. Whitson, and his disability came through without a hitch. That was a big burden lifted off us for John really took a hit on his retirement. We were now on to the undertaker. We procrastinated with this one. Christmas came, and we still didn't have this one done.

The girls came home for a few days during Christmas. We all made a special effort for little Harry. I was in constant prayer over the holiday for John was not doing well and was grumpy. He sat in his easy chair most of the time. The girls and I kept our spirits up and celebrated, but there was heaviness in our hearts. They hugged on their dad and teased him calling him a puss. We had a laugh or two and then back to reality after New Year's. More tests and more appointments were to come in January 2016.

John was progressively declining. His oxygen level had been raised to seven or eight continuous liters. Sleeping at night was horrible. I thought about moving into one of the other bedrooms, but felt I needed to be next to him at night. If he needed me or stopped breathing, I was there. I tried to keep him active and healthy, but time took its toll on him. The doctor told us this could happen. The old doubt kept creeping into my head about making it in time. I sat by the big picture window in a chair, talked to God, and asked him to help each morning. Watching your husband die slowly was unbearable. He would gasp for air if he over did any activity.

John's frustration with how hard it was to do even the little things usually ended in a swearing fit. He would become angry if I tried to help. Some things he just could not do because he didn't have enough air. Just tying his shoes became impossible. It wore on me daily, but my friends and family helped me cope by offering positive words through daily phone calls and prayers. It was incredibly hard to be positive twenty-four hours a day, but I tried to soak myself in scriptures and Christian television. Being an optimist was not easy for the atmosphere and mood was overwhelmingly depressing as we continually jumped through the hoops required for the possibility of getting on a transplant list. John was a trooper. He kept trying and that was all I asked of him. He was so spent and fragile, time was against us. The power of the Father, the Son, and the Holy Spirit and the prayers from those around us sustained us.

    Our friends Beverly and Rick and two of their children, Rhett and Shelby, helped us numerous times during the winter months on the farm. All of her children were excellent ropers. They attended many rodeo competitions in the late fall and spring. John couldn't get out or walk too far so Rick, Bev, Shelby, and Rhett helped us out with the new calves. Bev had grown up in Dodge City, Kansas. She was a true cowgirl. Rick worked for the largest cattle lot in the nation in Scott City. They knew more about cattle than I would ever know. One weekend the entire Weber family came over for a small rodeo at the Herzig farm. I loaded up the syringes with the vaccinations required for each calf. Next, the ear tags and the bands were readied to be placed on the male calves for castration.

    We all went out to the red milk barn and moved the calves into the coral. Rhett and Shelby cornered them and roped them one at a time. The dust was everywhere; calves fought against Rhett while he was picking them up and slamming them to the ground. Rick placed his foot on the neck and held it still. He vaccinated, tagged, and banded them one at a time. They got this accomplished in record time. It was nice to have all this help for this annual job. God had blessed me with wonderful Christian friends.

At times, I would go days without a good night's sleep. I would lay awake and listen to John breathe. He would stop breathing, and I would find myself punching him a little to get him breathing regularly again. He would wake up tired every day. It was a struggle, a big ordeal, to get ready to go anywhere. Taking a shower exhausted him. Bending over was almost impossible, so putting on socks put him over the top. His hearing was becoming worse because of the oxygen constantly moving through the tubing around his ears. Watching television with him was torture, so often times I retreated to the bedroom. It was so loud the neighbors could hear it and they lived a mile down on the next section line.

In February of 2016, we had been at the task of completing all the required tests for four and a half long months. We'd been told that a doctor in Texas was interested in our case and had been looking over John's records. This was the second opinion Dr. Mirza said he would pursue. Dr. Torres came to Oklahoma City to speak to the team. This would settle whether a transplant would be for one lung or two. There were more risks with a bilateral, but John had twenty percent function in the left lung and less than fifty percent in the right lung. It made sense to me he needed two lungs.

Just one more test to go in the early part of March. He would be nicotine free for six months and had passed all his tests after this one. We were getting close to getting on the list. It was what we hoped and prayed for each passing day. Dr. Mirza came in and talked to us about going to Texas. The surgical staff could not come to a unanimous decision about John's case, so Dr. Torres invited us to the University Of Texas Southwestern Medical Center in Dallas,

Texas. He was currently the chairman of the transplant department of pulmonologists for this medical center. He wanted us to come to UT Southwestern the third week in March for some further testing and a consult with him and some other doctors on the staff. Six months had passed, and we had all the tests completed. John had passed them all, yet he was not getting on a list. We had to go on this journey again to Texas. I felt like a dog that had jumped through the hoops only to be told no, not one dog treat. Time was on my mind. Didn't they realize we were running out of time? I could see it. John was ever so worse.

John wanted to give up at times. It was disheartening. Lance would call at the right time. God's alarm clock went off in his head, I thought. God used Lance to sustain us by praying and encouraging us along this journey. He would call and pray with us over the phone. We began thinking and praying about the donor family and including them in our group phone prayers even though we were not on a list.

Lance posted this prayer on Facebook in March 2016, reading it, I sobbed.

My command is this: Love each other as I have loved you. Greater love has no one than this: to lay down one's life for one's friends. (John 15:12-13 NIV) My family is waiting, watching, and praying for our Uncle John. Soon he will be on the list for a double lung transplant. This is filled with all kinds of swirling emotions, fear, anxiousness, doubts, and worry just to name a few. But as we get closer to this day when the call is made that a match for his transplant is here a thought arises. Someone, a stranger somewhere out there will have to die so John can live. The request: To those whose salvation is secure, to all the families that surround the Herzig family. Pray not only for our own family but also the family that will be giving a most precious and reluctant gift.

We did not even say or think we would not get on a list; we just kept the faith. It was the size of a mustard seed by now, but that was all it took according to the Bible. So Jesus said to them, "Because of your unbelief, for assuredly, I say to you, if you have faith as a mustard seed, you will say to this mountain, 'Move from here to there,' and it will move; and nothing will be impossible for you. However this kind does not go out except by prayer and fasting." (Matthew 17:20) *KJV*. God was in charge!

Lance did this exercise over the phone on a day that John and I truly needed it. We were to get a piece of paper and placed all of our concerns on it. In the middle of it, we wrote "God has this!" and gave it up to our heavenly Father that very moment. We placed it on the refrigerator, read it, and believed it every day. That paper still hangs on the refrigerator to this very day.

One morning I got up and looked into the mirror, and I suddenly looked old. The journey we were on had taken a toll on me. We had one last chore to accomplish before we went to Texas later this month and that was the undertaker. I wanted to get this done. Time was running out and this had to be finalized before anything happened. We had had the brochures and materials from the funeral home sitting on the kitchen counter for months. I was counting on the rapture so all of this silliness would not be necessary. I really didn't look at it until now, and I forced John to sit down with me to fill out his preparation plan. It was not as morbid as you might think. We both wanted to be cremated and our ashes scattered into the pond on our farm. Yes, we made some fish bait jokes. I would often say we need to stock our pond with some catfish. They are bottom feeders and would keep our tomb, so to speak, clean. If John would ignore me or just not answer me when I was talking, I yelled, "Hey, fish bait!" I laughed about it so that kept me focused and moving toward the ultimate goal of a task accomplished. The best part of this was that we would be dead and the family that carried on were the ones that would be emotional.

    The hard part was coming up with a service that was traditional and would fit our expectations. John wanted everyone to gather on the farm for drinks and goodbyes at the pond, but also a mass at the Catholic Church. He declared to be a new and changed Christian today. He said he understood now that a personal relationship with Christ was the important thing. He had been changed since the reunion. I hoped his plans would come off and that the kids could handle it. We had to list our favorite verses of the Bible, songs, flowers, pallbearers, and whom we would want residing over the service. What would it matter when you will only weigh about a pound of dust? We did the best we could and decided on the cheapest and shortest service available.

  We would be with our Lord and the mourners will be having drinks and saying goodbyes personally at the farm. The girls would not have their small inheritance stolen by the funeral home. We gave our work sheets to the undertaker, and he said your wishes will be done. Now that wasn't hard. Mission accomplished, for we had the last of the things done that our doctor told us to do at the beginning of this venture. It just took us longer than we thought it would. Now we were ready for the Dallas challenge in a few weeks.

CHAPTER FIVE
"The Takeoff"

We rolled up to the Holiday Inn in downtown Dallas and they were so nice to help us with all the oxygen machines and luggage. A five-dollar tip was not enough, but I didn't have anything smaller than a twenty on me. It was a long five-hour trip from the farm and we had to get up early to report to Clements University Hospital for the first of twenty scheduled tests that week. We would be there until Friday. We would have at least four tests a day and two consultations with doctors that week.

We believed Dr. Torres had our best interest at heart and brought us here and would help John get on a list soon. The school was actually hidden inside the heart of the medical district. Three very large hospitals were within blocks of each other. Huge complexes of medical buildings lined Harry Hines Boulevard. Ambulance sirens echoed constantly. The campus was spread out over the medical district with paid parking everywhere you visited. They charged three to five dollars a day for parking no matter where you were on the medical complex. We spent a lot of time at professional buildings one and two, which were connected by an atrium and a short hall. Once entering the building one the lab and imaging was right there for transplant patients. Across from this enormous lab were a physical therapy room and a pharmacy. Building two was offices of the different medical specialties such as lung, heart, and kidney.

We spent the most time on level six where the heart and lung transplant patients and candidates had appointments with the cardiac doctors or pulmonologists. We saw our first transplant coordinator, Jody

Hernandez, who went over the transplant protocol with us. She was very young and knowledgeable and didn't want to sound redundant. She knew we had been through the same consulting in Oklahoma City. She gave us a final list of what tests John had to complete this week. She reiterated the importance of seeking an air ambulance service. We lived too far away and had to reach the hospital within the three-hour window of transplantation. She was a contact we relied upon after returning home.

The financial coordinator, Evelyn Gomez helped us with our insurance company by getting an out of state contract so John could come to UT Southwestern if he were to become a transplant candidate. She also covered costs of the entire procedure and advised us to weigh out any changes to coverage as Medicaid eligibility approached. A social worker, Stacy Franz, explained the emotional roller coaster we were on and small support groups that were available. The last person was Francis Dang. She reviewed the nutritional information especially for diabetics. We spent two hours with this staff and they explained post-transplant procedures and what life would be like as there would be many changes to make. We heard there Texas version, and we did not cry this time. We had already run a marathon to get to this point. Fatigue had set in on us. There was a small issue with the insurance company since we were out of state, but a special contract was drawn up since the transplant institute in Oklahoma hadn't placed him on a transplant list, and Texas was trying to get us to that point.

    We returned to the hotel each evening with more and more material and list of things we would have to adjust to such as no cats, no feather pillows, no birds of any kind, no handling of fish or other animals, no swimming in lakes or ponds for the rest of your life. All meat was to be fully cooked and straws used for every glass. We lived on a farm so this would all take some adjusting. John couldn't be around animals, children, or adults that had been vaccinated in the past three weeks. No eating at buffets or using their eating utensils. Plastic ware and using a straw would be in order from now on. We were to sit away from crowds in restaurants and in the wintertime, isolation was encouraged. This meant we could not go to malls, churches, restaurants, family gatherings and any other place were lots of people were during the cold and flu season. This was little to ask if John could get a second chance at life.

This team had already performed five hundred fifty transplants. They do about seventy-to-one hundred lung transplants per year. The same for the heart transplants. They had done twenty or so last year in Oklahoma City, which was low volume in comparison. UT Southwestern was a transplant hub, which had a very large volume of transplants. The doctors had done so many they had seen most of the problems and complications that could occur. I felt confident knowing we were in the hands of surgeons who had done this surgical procedure many times.

This was a good thing. God sent us to UT Southwestern, and He would see to it that John had a chance at eventually getting new lungs. I clung to positive thoughts and felt encouraged by all the prayers from home while we were in Texas. The week ended, and I was anxious to return home. The enthusiasm of the medical personnel was contagious, and I went home thinking one day John would be back for new lungs. The last meeting on Friday was with the pre-transplant coordinator, Jody. She said not all the test results were back yet ,so the doctors could review them. She stated that John would be evaluated and voted on by the panel of medical personnel. Then we would get a call from her that John would be placed on the national transplant list. She wished us well and said she would call when she knew the findings of the panel. She said these things tended to happen quickly. We were in good spirits going home on Friday; God had answered another load of prayers. We just hoped they would call soon to tell us John was on a list. Hell, at this point being on a grocery list sounded good. I joke, of course.

My Christian friends were unrelenting about praying for John and me. I would text them that John needed prayers and instantly Bev, Geri, Martha, or Amie would send me a text full of encouragement with confirmation of many heart-felt prayers going up. Some days I felt sorry for God; His mail was overflowing. I had a team of prayer warriors like no other. This could actually be felt every day. My family and friends deserved the lion's share of praise for all that they had done. Words weren't enough to express the love I had for them when we were so far down in this valley. What a joy to know one has friends like these. John received cards and letters from Sunday school classes that held him up in prayer. They came from Kansas, Oklahoma City, Texas, and Arkansas. How could we ever repay so much kindness? I was overwhelmed with the love of God present in so many people I come face-to face with in this life. They have shielded me from loneliness, some cried with me, others laughed, but most importantly, they talked to God with me through so many prayers. My family and friends were the ones I reached out to when I returned from Dallas.

    It was a waiting game. I had always been terrible at waiting. This endeavor had tested my waiting skills and forced me to become patient at waiting. I found humor in some of the waiting. Not just the waiting to hear if John's on the transplant list, but the waiting in traffic, waiting for the doctors, or waiting in line at the Walmart pharmacy or just waiting in the waiting room had become less difficult or aggravating. This had a psychological effect on me. Seriously! We were home for only two days, and I was already wondering how long the waiting would be before we heard anything from Texas. How long before we're on a list? We were running out of time. This trip took a toll on John. My mind tortured me with him dying while waiting and other dark thoughts. I remembered a verse "Draw near to God, and He will draw near to you." (James 4:8) *KJV*

It was happening again, the doubting, and I knew prayer with someone was needed. We talked to Lance, and I told him how positive the Dallas trip had been and that they would let us know after the panel votes. We prayed for the donor family and prayed that the person who would give the lungs to John was a Christian. It made me cry to think others would feel such pain so we may know so much joy.

Your word is a lamp to my feet and a light to my path. (Psalm 119:115)
When I needed direction or comfort, the Bible was full of both. How do I thank my God that was so lovely? I was stronger when I was weak. I felt His arms about me. I basked in His glow. Three days had passed and the transplant coordinator Jody called John on his cell phone. John placed the call on speaker, so we could both listen what news she had to tell us.

"Congratulations! Mr. Herzig you will be placed on the national organ transplant list tomorrow morning. Pack your bags this has been known to happen quickly. You never know so just be ready." Jody explained.

Jody Hernandez hung up, and we smiled and exhaled. It finally happened. We were on the list. This had to be how a lottery winner felt. We sat in our easy chairs silent.

I turned to him and said, "Hey, good looking, were on a list. Praise His holy name," I said.

We were in line and waiting. Three days back from Dallas, and we made the list. Jesus died on a cross, was buried, and rose again in three days. What a difference three days made. I hugged John and said, "God is at work." The pit in my stomach was gone. We called the girls, the extended family, and friends who had been waiting to hear the happy turn of events. His name was placed on the list March 29th. This was exactly seven months to the day from our twenty-ninth wedding anniversary. *What a coincidence,* I thought to myself. Seven is God's perfect number, His fingerprint. He created the world in that amount of time. Thank you, Jesus, for Your Amazing Grace, I muttered to myself.

John and I had to carry our phones now at all times. The transplant team would call us on John's cell phone if donor lungs became available and viable. John's name, blood type, disease process, body size, how sick he was, and the LAS, Lung Allocation System, data were placed in the National United Network for Organ Sharing computer data base. This system determines the order in which lung offers are made to candidates awaiting transplantation. This organization allowed for fair and equal distribution of donor organs. The LAS method is based on a net benefit and will give priority for lung offers to those who are urgently in need of a transplant and who will receive the greatest benefit. We were to have our bags packed including all legal documents. We had just purchased a membership in an air ambulance transport company, EagleMed, for our entire household. This was the only option to get John to Dallas under the three-hour window.

The second recommendation we could not do because we lived too far away from the hospital. The team wanted us to join a support group that would help us in coping with the various issues and experiences before and after the transplant. My main job as his number one was to keep him moving and healthy so He wouldn't be bumped off the list. No pressure!

I felt so relieved that we had jumped this big hurdle that I believed a celebration was in order. I called the girls early in the week and asked them to come to dinner on Sunday evening. Katie and Harry lived in Moore and Abbie lived in Ponca City. It was a drive just for a dinner, but they were Daddy's girls. Spring was in the air although it was still chilly at night. Things were beginning to turn green and the winter wheat looked good this year. I doubted that a garden would be tilled this year. The grill and smoker were under the elm trees just north of the porch. I cleaned and made it ready to cook out. We would enjoy the screened in porch and have family time together. After all, John had endured so much so far, he needed this and some time with our grandson, Harry. John looked frail as he moved slowly pulling his oxygen behind him. He stayed in his easy chair with a blanket about his shoulders almost all of the time. He lounged in pajama pants most every day. Getting out on the porch would do him good. He sat in his easy chair waiting for the girls to show up for dinner. They had just arrived and I went out on the porch. John's cell phone rang, and he yelled at me to come quickly. I was hugging Harry and welcoming our daughters' home. I ran to the den to see what John was yelling about. The girls followed right behind me. He turned down the television and waited until I was standing in front of him to speak.

"It's the call," John shouted.

"You mean the, we have some lungs call?" I inquired.

"I'm going to put you on speaker." John told the lady.

It was the call, the lifesaving call that so many wait for and never lived to answer. I fell to my knees facing John sitting in his chair with my hands on his knees, and I stared into John's eyes and intently listened to the woman explain we would get four more calls before it was a go. We did not catch her name, but she spoke with an Asian accent, and it was hard to understand everything she was saying to us. We requested she repeat herself several times, as we could not grasp it because of her heavy accent. We are Okies and words are drawn out slowly.

The surgeon, the EagleMed flight operator, the hospital, and then, she would call again. We had so long to get on the flight while the team harvested the donor organs for transplantation. She explained and asked John if he would participate in the clinical trial using the ex-vivo technology, and she said if he would, they would have some lungs that would become viable in the next few hours using this technology.

"The lungs were high risk," she said.

I remembered some of the material that explained the donors had been in a traumatic situation such as a car accident, a stroke, or a gun shooting. Most of the donors were under sixty years of age. All were screened for viruses including HIV, hepatitis, and cytomegalovirus. I had nothing in my memory about this. What was ex-vivo?

"The risks of a dry run were still there, but he's a good match," she said.

Why couldn't we have some no risk lungs, I thought. John began squeezing my hand and looking in my eyes searching for an affirmation to all of this. My mind was trying to retrieve any past information about this new technology. I had to know more before I would say yes to this. This was my John!

He told the lady to hold for one moment and looked at me.

"Honey, I should take this opportunity," John said calmly.

He was sure and wanted me to know that everything was going to be okay. God had calmed him instantly and opened him to this extraordinary moment without any fear or doubt. There wasn't a calm cell in my body. We were at the crossroads of the most important decision regarding John living or dying and calm was not there for me. I nodded an okay, then, placed my head in his lap. He stroked my hair with his huge hands. The girls were leaning over the back of the easy chair stunned, but smiling and shook their heads to indicate to go for it. I was in a state of excited shock. John got back on the phone.

"Yes, I will do it! He excitedly told her.

John hung up the phone, and we all paused a moment; nothing but silence, then all hell broke loose. We all jumped up and down with excitement.

We hadn't packed a bag. We didn't have enough oxygen to take with us if it was a dry run. We didn't have any cash on us, and the girls decided they were going with the clothes on their backs. We sent them with the credit card to gas up. John called his brother, sister, and Lance about the good news. I called Larry's Oxygen and got an on-call delivery man out to the farm within the hour with enough oxygen machines and bottles. The kind man brought out and loaded what we'd need to return to Enid if it was a dry run. I began throwing clothes into an empty suitcase sitting on the floor of the bedroom. It had been there since we had returned from Dallas. The phone rang; everyone froze, held their breath, and yelled for John to answer his phone. It was EagleMed flight team telling us they would be at Woodring Airport at ten o'clock. John handed me his phone and stepped into the shower. The rushing atmosphere took a toll on John. I helped him gather his clothes and helped him into the shower. He was gasping for the next breath and bent over. The third call came from the hospital confirming the ambulance would meet the medical flight at Love Field and take John to the ER at Clements University Hospital. The last call came from the Asian lady. It was a go!

My heart was pounding with excitement; I knew John had a million things going on in his mind. I prayed that he was not afraid. I couldn't become emotional I was focused with getting everything including John loaded into the truck. Thank God, Abbie was home. She and Katie were strong enough they could get him in the truck. He was packed and sitting in his easy chair. He needed another bottle of oxygen hooked up, and I went to get this last chore completed. I needed a prayer to keep my strength but it had to wait. Abbie helped me get John out to the truck on the driveway; he was weak and unbalanced from his breathing difficulties. I was actually out of breath with all the hustling, and it felt good to be seated in the truck.

"Are you ready? Let's go get you on God's flight, Sweetie," I said.

As we headed to the airport, I made a mental checklist of things we had to do and checked them off when I realized that they were all finished.

"The paperwork," I said, "Is the bag in the truck?" I anxiously asked.

The bag contained all the legal documents required of any transplant patient. It had a power of attorney, a DNR (do not resuscitate), the funeral director's phone numbers, and other documents such as insurance cards inside and I carried it at all times. I had to be legally prepared no matter where we were going for John could undergo complications at any time.

John's medications crossed my mind. *Did I have all he needed?* I did not know what John had packed in his suitcase, but it was loaded in the truck. The many responsibilities and having to remember for both of us took a toll on the spouse of a transplant patient. Being in the throes of a situation this emotional, my thinking had become somewhat foggy. The ordeal of getting him on the flight took its toll.

After John boarded his flight for Dallas, I began driving robotically south on I-35 to begin our journey. I checked the rear view mirror and made sure Abbie was still behind me. I talked to Lance and he was on his way from Ft. Worth to the hospital ER in Dallas, and he would meet the ambulance arriving from Love Field. I did not want John to be alone at any time before surgery. John's flight would be there in a little over an hour. Lance would be there in plenty of time. I shared with Lance the overwhelmingly calm demeanor that God had placed over John. He was great and I was a wreck.

"Please call me when he gets there," I told him.

Lance assured me that I would receive a call as soon as he arrived. The plane should be on the ground about eleven o'clock, so it would be hours before I arrived at the hospital. We arrived in Oklahoma City and picked up Katie and Harry at their apartment. Katie and Harry had driven on to Moore, Oklahoma while Abbie and I got John on his flight. Next we pulled into the Wal-Mart stopped and grabbed a few clothes, a toothbrush, and something to eat. We had not eaten supper, and it caught up with us. Fast food was okay. I was hungry. As we were checking out the phone rang. It was Lance.

"There's someone here that would like to say hello," Lance said.

He was there safely and in the pre-operating room.

"The flight down was smooth, and they are getting me ready, John said.

It will take some time. They had to give me anti-rejection meds and some other drugs through an IV. The lungs have arrived and were placed in the ex-vivo machine."

I forgot about that. This machine was something with the clinical trial. I was so nervous when the lady called, I didn't listen carefully to them explain that part of the procedure.

"Everyone is really nice here and taking good care of me, Honey. It's all still a go is what Dr. Peltz told me. He's the surgeon. When you get here come in the main hospital entrance, tell them your name, and they will bring you up to my pre-operative room on the third floor," John said.

"They won't begin until I get there, right? I will get to see you before you go into surgery? I have to see you, honey, make them wait," I said.

"No, it would be sometime was what Dr. Peltz said. Don't worry, honey," John said.

All was going well, we still had three and one half hours of driving left, but I knew it would go fast. I passed the news on to the girls behind me and kept heading south.

Surprisingly, the traffic was not too bad in Dallas at four-thirty in the morning. We were rolling into the entrance of Clements University Hospital and had the valet park our cars. We went to the first desk as we entered the building.

They assisted us to the third floor and took us all back to John's room. Lance was there snoozing in a chair. John was asleep. I hadn't even felt sleepy, and it was night before last that I had slept. I kissed John's cheek, and he awoke.

"I'm getting a little snooze while I can, John whispered. The doctor will be back in to talk to us and let us know how the lungs are doing."

I got into my document bag and pulled out the information the transplant team had given us. There it was an article about Dr. Bajona and the ex-vivo lung perfusion technology clinical trials. UT Southwestern was one of sixteen medical centers across the country participating in a national clinical trial of the ex-vivo technology. UT Southwestern was the only medical center in Texas in the trials.

They placed the lungs into a clear dome-shaped machine that evaluated the pressure in the blood vessels of the lungs, ventilated the lungs, and perfused them with a special solution for a few hours. They even measure the ability of the lung tissue to stretch and expand and the function of gas exchanges. This technology reconditioned the donor lungs and helped the physicians determine the viability of the lungs before transplantation. This all seemed like it was from outer space. The machine looked like one of the cars in cartoons that the Jetsons used to drive. It sounded like something NASA had created. So, this was the reason for the waiting. The doctors were watching and evaluating the lungs that would be placed into John. I guessed they would call it off if this machine didn't make the lungs viable. There was not any information on the number of people who had taken lungs from this technology or how successful it had been.

Nurses were regularly in and out. I was frightened after reading all the information in the bag. Around six-thirty Dr. Bajona came in and explained how things were progressing and that we were getting closer. The doctor was Italian and had a beautiful accent as he spoke to us.

"What part of Italy do you call home?" I asked.

"Tuscany," he stated. "I don't know what I'm doing in Texas."

We all laughed.

The doctor said, "If for any reason the team got into surgery, and they didn't think the lungs were right, they would stop, and it would be deemed a dry run."

Apparently, this happened a lot, and he wanted us to be prepared to go back home to wait for the next call. I almost yelled, don't you know what we've been though in the last twelve hours or so? Are you kidding me! I couldn't go through all those emotions again. I'd have a heart attack.

Well, Abbie lightened things up a bit. I saw her take something out of the box on the wall as the doctor exited the room. She grabbed a sterile glove out of the box on the wall and began blowing it up. The glove was half way blown up, but Abbie lost it, and it flew around the room. We all started laughing. She pulled another, blew it up three times the normal size, and tied it off. It looked like an enormous, blue rooster comb. She batted it over to me; I was sitting in the chair at the head of John's bed. I batted it back to her, and we proceeded to play a volleyball game. John was the net. Jordan and Lance became involved, so we had two on each team. A nurse came in to check on the IV line. The blue rooster ball came her way, and she batted it over the net. The medical staff had stopped to play with us. That was neat. I overheard her say to the other nurses at the desk, "Now, those are my kind of people." For just a moment, God directed us in play allowing a moment of laughter in this unsettling situation. I guess the Herzig family started lung transplant volleyball as a preoperative exercise. It was strangely light-hearted the whole time we were waiting.

It was now seven-thirty, and it was time to check out the cafeteria for breakfast. Breakfast was the most important meal of the day so Abbie and Jordan went looking for it. They were gone ever so long, then bounced back in, and announced that this cafeteria was "the bomb."

"Oh! Really bad, eh?" I teased.

"No, Mom! It's a gourmet food stop."

I couldn't eat. My stomach was off, but coffee could keep my motor running a few extra miles. John couldn't have anything. I told him I was going for a cup and would be right back. I stepped into the third floor waiting room and a long table adorned with complimentary coffee and all the necessary condiments awaited me. This was nice. I didn't have to be away from John that long. Time dragged along it seemed, maybe because I was beginning to slow down a bit. Two hours had passed, and we kept asking every nurse that entered the room if we were getting closer. Of course they all said yes. Pressure was rising within me as the time drew near to say goodbye, and I fought the tears welling up in my eyes.

The doctor came back by around ten-forty-five and said, "It won't be long, and we will go into surgery.

"Even after we get into surgery," he said, "if it is not perfect, we will not proceed."

He then told us us that a nurse would call from the operating room during the surgery to keep us informed. The nurse came in and placed some drowsy medicine into his IV line and left. I held John's hand and stroked his arm. I looked into his baby blue eyes. We just silently stared at each other. I did not want to let go. In my mind, I asked myself, *would I be able to let go? It won't be much longer. I need a letting go lesson, God.* I tried to memorize his hands and thought about how many years I'd held them. I kept thinking about what was going to happen to John.

Twenty-five minutes later two nurses with surgical masks came in and announced that it was time to go. The family gathered around John's bed and held hands for a word of prayer. The nurses bowed their heads too. Lance led us in the Lord's Prayer. The girls and Lance said their goodbyes and left John and me alone for just a moment. The nurses stepped out as well to give us privacy. I began to tear up as I love you came out at the same time. I gave him one last kiss.

"I know it will be alright, so please be here when I wake up," he whispered.

"I'll be right here, and you will be so much better. I said. "God will be right there in the operating room looking after you, honey."

Oh, I couldn't let go, but I knew everyone was waiting. I hugged him one last time and held his eyes until the nurses came back into the room. With that, the nurses rolled the bed into the hall down through two large double doors to the operating room. The pit in my stomach had returned, and it made me sick. I took in a big breath, wiped the tears away, picked up my bag and my Bible and I was on my way to the waiting room right outside the preoperative rooms. Everyone was waiting for me and led me to a place we could settle in for the day. There was a place to play cards and to plug and charge your phones. I just needed the family near and words were not necessary. They sensed this so they let me have some time to myself on the couch nearby.

     I sat down and closed my eyes, but the tears would not stop. I took in a huge breath and said aloud, "Oh God, watch over John." I had lost control of the water works and the tears kept rolling down my face. I bowed my head and closed my eyes for a moment of solitude. This was the moment in my life that God asked me to believe and to trust in him totally. It was my moment to free fall into the arms of Almighty God. Trusting wholeheartedly for the first time in my life, and I was scared to death. John had already had this realization the moment he said yes to the lifesaving call.

CHAPTER SIX
"The Flight"

I opened my eyes again, I realized I had John's phone and mine and a lot of people to text between the both of them. I sent a text to my family first and then to my girlfriends for immediate prayer for he had gone into surgery. I looked at the date and time on the iPhone, and it was April 4, 2016, eleven ten in the morning. I suddenly realized this was the seventh day on the transplant list. Mrs. Hernandez called and placed us on the list on the twenty-ninth day of March. This was the day John would get new lungs and would give him an extended time in this life. Also, it was exactly seven months ago to the day on September 4, 2015 that we walked into the Nazih Zuhdi Transplant Institute for his first appointment. Seven is God's fingerprint. I was amazed how God had total control over our lives and handled this situation with his perfect timing. What were the odds of this timing? I began texting that John was in surgery and it could take six to ten hours depending on any complications. I solicited prayers from everyone on both phones. We had a lot of friends and family, so God would be inundated with requests about John this day.

The waiting room seemed to fill up with a lot of people, so I changed to a more comfortable chair with more room for the girls to play cards. My sister, Leesa, arrived from Houston to sit with us; Lance headed back to Ft. Worth to get some rest and let his wife, Carrie, come to the hospital for a while. Carrie was watching Harry and Noah, a cousin just six months younger. Harry had his cousin as a playmate during this unsettling time. We knew we would be in the waiting room for an extended stay, so the girls played cards to help pass the time. I was focused and not in the mood for games. I had John in my thoughts constantly. The surgeons had John's life in their hands, and God was guiding their every move. I went through the operation in my mind several times just like they told us they would proceed.

The surgeons make an incision across his chest, which extended from under one arm to the other below the breast line. They would saw the sternum in half, and raise the rib cage up out of the way as if opening the hood of a car. They move the heart aside and place him on a bypass machine while they remove the lungs. They remove one lung at time carefully taking out all the scar tissue. This takes an enormous amount of time. Once the old lungs are removed, they cannot put the old ones back, they are discarded as waste. The new lungs have to be placed into John's chest cavity one at a time. They place his heart back into place and take him off of bypass. The new lungs have to begin functioning properly or John will surely die. Once they jump-start the lungs, they lower the hood back down and close. This all seemed simple running through it in my mind, but it is an extremely difficult operation with teams of doctors in the operating room. One nurse told me thirteen or fourteen people were in the operating theater during a lung transplant. I didn't know what would happen when he got out of surgery or what to expect that wasn't included in our training. I did know that he would be in the intensive care unit for some time. I lost my train of thought and popped back to the conversation my sister was having with the girls. She knew I only needed someone close by and that conversation at this time was unnecessary with her oldest sister.

My cell phone rang abruptly which startled me. My thoughts went negative for just a moment thinking the worst before I actually talked to the person on the phone. It was a UT Southwestern phone number.

"Hello," I said.

"Is this Mrs. Herzig?" she asked.

"Yes," I replied.

It was a nurse from the operating room to update me on John's progress. Her voice resonated with a reassuring tone as she began reporting the status of the procedure.

"The surgeons have the left lung in place and are fixing to proceed with the right lung. There hasn't been any complications thus far and the surgery is going well. The operation will continue for another three hours at best estimate then I will call you at that time. Do you have any questions?"

"No, thank you for the update," I said.

Why didn't I tell her the truth? I thought. I had a million questions, but I was too stressed to remember to ask her. I was a limp rag. I was so exhausted. I hung up, turned around, and saw the faces in our group fixated on me during the phone call. They were eagerly The waiting to hear the news. I reiterated what the nurse had told me with the group, and you could hear sighs of relief. The pit in my stomach was ever present. The visual pictures in my mind of John lying on the table with one lung made me sick. I sat down and shook all over with nervousness. I glanced at the time, and it was a little after three o'clock. Only four hours had passed. I was exhausted but there was no relaxing this day. I told everyone that I needed to be alone, and I was going for a walk. The girls found a couple of long couches in a corner and took a nap.

    I finally took a look around and found this hospital was beautiful, with ten floors each floor opening up into this huge atrium of solid glass. I could look over the railing and see the ground floor. I could also see the fountains outside, and I felt all the angels about this place as the sunlight poured into

and filled the atrium with light. Waiting rooms filled the third floor with families occupying all of them. *It must be a great day for organ operations*, I thought. They were waiting for one of God's miracles. I visualized thousands of little bubbles rising up in the atrium with prayers in each one of the bubbles. *It was Monday,* I thought, *and everyone must receive an organ on Monday.*
 All the doctors had had a wonderful weekend, they were rested, and now it was time for some miracles. You could feel God's army of angels going about doing His will for all here in this place. Fifty operating rooms must have been back there. Each family surely had their own stories and horrors they had been living, and now it was Monday, a new week, a new day of hope. I was ready for my life to change, and normal would do just fine. I went in to the ladies room, and after glancing at myself in the mirror, I decided it was time to put on some war paint. I washed my face, put

on some makeup, and actually felt refreshed and human again. I slowly made my way back to where the family was waiting.

While I was away John's older brother, Jim and his sister, Barbara had arrived from Oklahoma and were sitting with Leesa. I told them the latest news. One lung was in place and they were working on the right lung now. That news was two hours ago, and I didn't expect any more news for hours to come. I was glad my sister was there for talking was not for me at this time. Someone suggested they go to dinner in the cafeteria and most went down. I couldn't leave the waiting area that was close to the surgical rooms. I had to know about John, and I felt better just sitting close by. I saw numerous doctors come out in their surgical scrubs to visit with families. I saw the relief in their faces as the doctors would talk to them. I hoped our doctor would come out soon, and our family would receive wonderful news. Another hour flew by and the family was back in the sitting area when the second call came from the operating room. I knew it was them. It was the same number as before. I was desperate to hear what they would say.

"Hello"

"Mrs. Herzig?"

"Yes, yes this is she," I said.

"The right lung is in place, and the lungs are functioning; the doctors are about ready for closing."

"Oh, my God," I said out loud, "they are finished?"

"Yes," the nurse told me.

I turned and faced the family and said, "Praise almighty God, he has made it through the surgery."

I had never experienced such relief. You could hear sighs of relief from everyone seated in our family group. We all hugged each other and tears of joy consumed us. A grey-headed lady seated to the left of me smiled and waved at me. She had heard the good news and the happy noises, we all made. Smiles and laughter replaced worry and concern. The lady had a group of four ladies with her all afternoon. They were waiting on a doctor that had been in surgery all day. Her husband, Wendell, had a massive heart attack, and they had not determined what they should do in his case. I finally, introduced myself and she said her name was Elizabeth King.

"I think the doctor we were waiting on was operating on your husband," she said.

"We will know shortly" I replied.

I told her I would pray for her husband and that I had to go to a different floor. The Herzig family gathered their things to go upstairs. John would be sent to the intensive care unit on the ninth floor. The nurse said that the doctors would talk to me there in just a while. We were to go on up to the waiting room, and John would be taken up momentarily.

It was after six o'clock now and the relief rolled over me; I was a different person. God had brought him through and He dragged me through as well. I was not a brave little Indian. I had had my weak moments. It was as if I had run a marathon, and I was now bent over catching my breath. I think a tear rolled down my cheek. I told my Father, thank you right out loud. I glanced at my watch. Seven hours ago, I was trembling with fear, but now I was trembling with overwhelming joy. I just realized the operation had taken seven hours. That's right another thing with God's perfect timing. Seven, God's fingerprint, kept turning up. I picked up my bag and my Bible and headed to the elevator with a parade of family following. Eight in our party, squeezed into the elevator and up we went to the ninth floor.

The waiting room was right off the elevator with a big sliding glass door leading to the ICU hall. We had to be buzzed in to gain entry. A locked metal gate last night had given me some trouble, and now I was hoping this sliding glass door wouldn't. The nurses had a huge circular desk area where medical staff gathered around and could go down any of three or four halls to ten or more ICU private rooms. Each room had sliding glass doors and a scrub room through which to enter first.

The nurses and doctors went in and scrubbed up before entering any room. They all wore masks, gloves, and gowns and changed them each time they entered a patient's room. The personnel wore navy blue scrubs with embroidered UT Southwestern on the left upper side of their scrubs and the doctors adorned their white starched coats with an id badge. It was like a war protection area for germs. No germs were getting in, period.

Each room had a computer connected to a machine, and all the wires hooked up to the patient ran to this machine. The patient's vitals and other things were on the computer, as well as, the monitor above the patient that constantly updated and gave the medical staff information regarding the patient. Someone on the staff was in the room with the patient at all times. The nurses were uniquely trained to care for lung transplant recipients and worked twelve-hour shifts. They communicated any and all concerns to the next nurse. Nothing got past these professional ladies. They had a direct line with the pulmonologists, and the doctors were there in an instant if the nurses thought there might be a problem. Other halls were heart, liver, and kidney transplant patients. Each nursing staff had specifically trained staff for those transplant patients. I'd never seen anything like this. Everything's bigger in Texas, so they say. Boy, this was something.

The entire family was sitting in the waiting area, talking to each other, and texting to friends. I texted on both phones to friends and family about John's great news. A nurse came through the sliding glass door and called my name. I went over.

"We're getting John settled into the ICU. You can see him for a few minutes tonight," she said.

"What about my daughters?" I asked.

"Yes, only two at a time. You can only observe him through the glass, okay?" No one except the attending nurse and doctor can scrub up and enter his room," she explained.

I followed the nurse through the door, walked down the hall to where the nurse stopped and pointed to the room. I turned and looked in. My mouth was wide open, my face expressionless. I placed my hands on the glass, and I just stared. The nurse was telling me something but I was fixated on John. I could barely see him beneath all the machines that were hooked up to him. The nurse inside the room stood behind a computer facing towards John. He was not awake. John had two large tubes down his throat. I suddenly realized he was on a ventilator. He told me he never wanted to be on a ventilator. I was becoming upset, and the nurse came to the sliding door and opened it ever so slightly.

"Why is he on a ventilator?" I asked the nurse. "Don't the new lungs work efficiently?"

"Yes, but this just helps him for a few days."

"What is your name?" I inquired.

"Katy," she said smiling.

"Oh, I have a Katie too." I said.

"I hear you are from Enid, Oklahoma. I am too," she smilingly said.

He was okay but too still for me to feel comforted. I stared and looked at John for the longest time before I realized someone was talking again.

I took my eyes off John and turned to her. "You are kidding me."

"I am Katy Henson. I know your nieces and nephews from attending Oklahoma State University. My dad has had a construction company in Enid for years."

What were the odds that John's nurse was from our hometown and had attended his alma mater. She knew the Herzig cousins that were there. The Herzig name had been on the OSU campus since 1945. John's father and mother both attended college there, as well as, John and all of his siblings. This was definitely a God thing.

"I'll take really good care of John," Katy said. "The doctor will be here in a few moments to answer all of your questions."

Katy closed the crack in the door. I could only watch John through the glass, for now. I could see him breathing or the ventilator breathing for him. The great almighty God brought John through this operation. It was a miracle. There had to be many guardian angels about this place. How could anyone endure the entire brutal process, and the operation without angels guarding them? They were doing God's business. I felt weak and tired as if I had come out of a sauna. I leaned my forehead against the glass and the emotion pent up for so long got the better of me. I just wept.

A nurse concerned came over. She placed her arms about my shoulder for reassurance. The nurse told me the doctor was coming down the hall to answer any questions that I might have at this time. She returned to the medical station as the doctor began to speak.

"Mrs. Herzig, John is doing extremely well after the transplant. He will not be awake for the next three days." You must observe him through the glass for that period of time," Dr. Torres explained.

"No one told me about this part of his recovery," I said.

"He will be brought out of the induced coma for a very short time and then back to sleep for a few days," he stated. "We don't want him pulling at the ventilator hose and feeling any pain. They tend to try to talk, as well, and he needs to be still for now."

"That makes sense and I understand, Doctor," I said.

"He is doing extraordinarily well. The lungs look good. He has tubes in both lungs to drain the fluid, and he will need to be given high doses of anti-rejection medicine and steroids. The lungs need a little extra help at first and the ventilator will allow John to rest and not have to work too hard breathing with his new lungs. I would request that family observe him outside the glass for the first few days. When he is brought out of the induced coma, we will let you scrub up and be in the ICU room with us. He will be coming off of some high powered medicine and will hallucinate at times," Dr. Torres explained.

This drug was Propofol, which had ended the life of a celebrity not too long ago. John was in *la la land* and didn't know it. I pressed my face to the glass.

"I'm here, honey," I muttered. "I wish I could give you a kiss and a hug."

Besides the ventilator hose, he had a small hose down his nose and a catheter line below with IV lines in both arms and the drain tubes in each of the lungs. If he were awake, he would be in excruciating pain.

"Rest, honey. I will be back in the morning," I whispered. "We will get through this together with the loving help of God."

I returned to the waiting area, and I tried to prepare Katie and Abbie before they went back to see their Daddy. I explained and described all the wires going to two different machines and the many tubes coming out of his body. I thought they were prepared to go back and view him through the glass. When they returned, they had an onslaught of question.

"Will Daddy be awake before we have to go home?" Katie asked.

"Why does Dad have the ventilator? He can breathe, right?" Abbie asked.

"Yes, Katie, in three days the doctors will bring him out of the induced coma. We will scrub up and get to go into his room while the doctors wake him up. Abbie, the ventilator allows Daddy to rest some, and his lungs don't have to work as hard." I explained.

Our conversation was reassuring to the girls, and they were not as anxious about their Daddy. I must admit they both had been extremely helpful and mature for their years during this devastating time in our lives.

Proud doesn't even come close to my description of these young women.

Barbara and Jim went back for a few minutes. I was sitting there texting the entire world that John came through the surgery and that thousands of prayers had been answered today. John's siblings came back and said goodbyes then headed back to Enid. I promised them I would keep them informed as to his progress. There was no telling how long John would be hospitalized.

No one on the pre-transplant team discussed how long John could be in the hospital. I just supposed each case was different, and John was in part of a clinical trial. I had read a mountain of material, but I needed a list for all the things I didn't know. *My God, that could take a large tablet.* I smiled at that thought. I could just hear my gang of friends say the Indian has gone nuts. A professional might have thought I was on the brink if he could hear my thoughts.

The pilot on this flight suddenly communicated to the passengers. This is the Captain speaking, "The turbulence we have been experiencing has subsided. We have now climbed to thirty-three thousand feet and all the stormy weather is now below us. You may now, move about the cabin. Relax and enjoy the remainder of your flight."

The time was close to 10:00 p.m. I was feeling the exhaustion. I had been up and moving since Sunday morning. It was now Monday night. It had been twenty-four hours since I left the airport in Enid. I called the Holiday Inn a few blocks away; they had one suite left. I grabbed my bag and my Bible and we were off. We retrieved the cars from the valet and headed to the hotel. The girls made out the sleeper sofa and one slept on the other queen bed. They watched television while I took a shower. They would soon follow but wanted me to get some rest. I slept as soundly as if I were a member of the rock or stone family. I was in the same position in the morning as when I laid down that night. I went to the mirror and stared. I had Bette Davis eyes. It's a good thing John was in a coma; my appearance could scare him to death. John had been in the fight of his life and had won thanks to a wonderful, loving God.

It was around eight am, and I needed to get to the hospital so I told the girls I would meet them there. I wanted to catch a doctor and really find out how John had progressed through the night. I didn't expect anything spectacular but hoped he had had a stable night. The nurses had my cell phone number and were to call if John's condition changed in any way. No calls meant an expectation he was doing well.

The shift change brought many new faces. John had a new nurse when I arrived. A female doctor was examining him. The curtains were closed, so I couldn't see what they were actually doing. I could, however, see her high heels. The nurse saw me, waved, and put up her wait just one-moment hand at me. After a few minutes, the doctor came from John's room and introduced herself. Doctor Jessica Mullins was young and an enterprising person. She had long straight dark hair and a beautiful smile when she used it. She was on the list of pulmonologists that would care for John.

"Your John is a rock star," she said. "He is doing fine. I'm a little concerned about his heart rhythm, but I will send the cardiac doctor by to see him later this morning."

She stated that his heart was beating a little fast but they had medicine that would help this, and that it wasn't unusual after a lung transplant. She would come by again late this evening and consult with the cardiac doctor about John. I could only stare at John through the glass. He never moved, but the machines told us he was breathing. I stared and watched for any movement just hoping he knew I was there with him. My legs grew tired and sore from standing, so I returned to the waiting area by the elevators.

I had my bag and my Bible, so I sat down to read. The waiting area was completely empty, filled only by God, His Word, and me. He is the only one who knew what John and I had been through all these months. He was the only one who knew the outcome. Praise laid on my heart and mind for this day, and that was what I began telling the Lord.

You never left us, and You never forsook us. You have taken care of all John's needs, and it was a miracle of Yours. You placed people in our paths to comfort us, to sustain us, and to renew our faith each day. Your timing was always perfect. I thank You this morning for Your love and Your miracles. I pray You will comfort the family of the person who gave John his new lungs. I pray they will feel Your love this day. I pray this special person is with You at this moment. I have never been so grateful in my life, Lord, for Your loving kindness. Amen

I opened my Bible and read from the Word of God my favorite passage; its page was worn with wear. "Ask and it will be given to you; seek and you shall find; knock and it shall be opened up to you." (Matthew 7:7) *KJV*. I asked for John to be restored and it was done. God had put him in the fire and molded him into something new. Rereading a verse in Job hit so very close to home. "When he has tested me, I shall come forth as gold. (Job 23:10) *KJV*. I felt we, as a family, had come through this experience and it had forever changed us. People all over the world who have never tasted the fire in this life, I was truly sorry for them. They will never know the great joy of being rescued or saved. I'm reminded that we're just passing through on our way to eternity and headed to a promised mansion in Paradise with Jesus. At this moment, I was overwhelmed by the awesomeness of our loving God.

I snapped back to the waiting room, and it had filled up with many families who had loved ones just out of surgery. I noticed Liz and her daughter Marty had come in this morning and sat down across the room. I walked over and sat down by Elizabeth.

"How's Wendell this morning?" I inquired.

"The doctors are still trying to decide what to do," she said. "They still have him opened up and cannot close until they figure it out. He has one chamber that doesn't work right, and he's on a bypass until they consult some other professionals. He's in a coma."

"I will be praying for Wendell and you," I told her.

Elizabeth lived in a small town about thirty minutes to the east of Dallas. She spoke with that Texas draw. I shouldn't talk for I have the West Texas twang to my voice. I had a connection instantly to her, and I thought God had given me another person to befriend and to comfort. I excused myself, went to the hall, and called the girls.

It was already lunchtime and the girls were not here yet. A quick call to them and a message to meet me in the gourmet cafeteria, to use Abbie's phrase, got them in gear. Our phones had so many messages on them that I had to stop and answer texts and updated them all on John's progress. I typed a generic message on both phones and sent it out to innumerable people. I asked a few friends to relay my message on Facebook to cut down on the messaging I would need to complete. When I finished, I headed to the cafeteria downstairs.

The gourmet cafeteria was exactly as Abbie described it. They had a pizza line, full meal and entrée line, a hamburger grill line, and a salad display that would shame most restaurants. The array of dessert offerings of cake, pie, and cookies was sinful. Yes, I had a piece of cake. The girls loaded up, and we had a lovely meal together. Smiles were back, laughter too. We had been a long time in the pressure cooker, and I let go enjoying the moment, my daughters, and God's sunshine. The seating choices were inside or outside on the east side of the hospital and windows let God's light in everywhere.

The girls were going to stay with me all week. They wanted to explore and find a Wal-Mart to get some things for the hotel room. Drinks and such were very expensive, so they were going to smuggle in their own stuff. The girls began playing a card game, Phase Ten, and asked me to play. We would take turns going back and checking on John through the glass and played cards all afternoon. I told them to go back to the hotel to swim or relax, and I would join them as soon as I had talked to the doctor.

I was really tired today and I needed to just relax and sleep at the hotel. It was close to six o'clock, so I went back to tell the nurse she could contact me by phone if she needed to, but I was going to the hotel. There were two doctors in with John, and they seemed to agree on something, and Dr. Mullins came out to talk to me.

"The medicine is not doing the job of regulating John's heart rhythm," Dr. Mullins said. "I need your permission to shock John's heart back into normal rhythm. He should be having seventy-two beats per minute. Right now, he is in double time or better. She pointed out the heart monitor through the window; it read one hundred sixty-four.

"His heart is racing, then," I said.

"Yes, and we have given it enough time on the medicine. It's not having an effect on the heart rate. Doing this, shocking him, there are some risks like stroke or heart attack, but they are very slight." She said.

"You are going to use the paddles and shock him?" I asked.

"Yes, and he is so out of it, he will not remember it," Dr. Mullins said.

"Is this unusual? Can he die?" I asked.

"It is not unusual and there is always a risk of dying. Your husband is in *afib*. We need to shock his heart into normal rhythm," Doctor Mullins said. "You will have to sign some papers that are ready for you at the nurse's station."

I had been under pressure so long that my decision-making skills were slow. I stood there with no one else to help me make this decision. So the counselor mode in me checked in with the questions I needed to make an informed decision at least.

"What will happen if we don't shock him?" I asked quickly.

"This is very hard on John's heart and he already has damage on his right side. A heart attack could occur," she said.

With those words, I asked, "Where do I sign?"

Doctor Mullins put her arm around my shoulders and assured me it would be okay.

"I will come out right afterwards," she said, "and you can stand right here behind the glass. It won't take long, and I believe it will do the job."

She entered the room; they pulled a cart inside and drew the curtains. I tried to hear any voices, but the glass was so thick nothing was audible. I asked God for His assistance holding my head in my hands. I had this picture in my mind of John's body bouncing up and then down like in the movies. I couldn't imagine the pain with all the stitches from the operation. I was so glad he was asleep. He would not remember it, which was what the doctor said. I was counting on it. He was in a coma-like sleep, so how could he know what was going on. I'd have hell to pay if he did remember. After ten minutes, Doctor Mullins came out.

"He's got rhythm," she said.

I was so relieved. Doctor Mullins was from Georgia and she was a corker. She was delightful and candid which was my kind of doctor. I was building a wonderful trusting relationship with her.

"This will probably do it," she said, "I will see him again tomorrow." The nurses will call if he goes back into *afib*.

With that reassurance from the doctor, I decided to call it a night. Tomorrow was the third day, and I wanted to be rested for the awakening. God escorted me through another fun filled day at the hospital and was seeing me home to the hotel.

The morning of the third day, I popped out of bed and ordered up coffee. War paint had to be on the face today. This would be the day I could talk to John and reassure him all was well. I couldn't wait to see those baby blues. I would be scrubbing up and going into the glass room in the ICU. The girls had to get going as well for they wanted to be part of this today. I got to the hospital, and I began playing it out in my head. I was so nervous; I looked like I was in the movie *M.A.S.H.* with everything they made me wear. I was standing at the foot of the bed. The doctors messed with the IV lines, stood back and waited for two minutes before asking John to open his eyes. Nothing happened for the longest time. He moved a little.

"There's a tube in your throat to help you breathe. We will try to take it out in just a little bit," the doctor said.

John was irritated. The doctor nodded to let me know it was okay to speak. I began to speak, and he calmed down a bit.

"Everything was successful," I slowly said. "You have been asleep for a few days, and they want you to refrain from talking now, so let me do all the talking." Katie and Abbie are here and want to see you in just a while. You have a tube to help you breathe easier for today, and then they will take it out. The doctors and nurses have been superior and you're recovering nicely. The girls are coming in to see you now. Don't talk; you let them talk to you. The doctors will let you go back to sleep, and I will see you tomorrow. I will be right here, honey. You rest easy.

    John began to tear up when I walked to the door and allowed the girls to enter. I could see them talking through the door window. I stayed inside the scrub room while they talked to him. They did not stay long, and I went back in for the last time that day. John was frightened with so many machines hooked up to him. He couldn't move his head because of the tube down his throat. His eyes were focused up at the ceiling. The tears kept rolling down the sides of his face. His eyes appeared sleepy and dull. *It must be the drugs,* I thought. The doctors said he was progressing as expected. He would need to get up and about on the fourth day, so they would take the tubes out early tomorrow. They put him back to sleep until then. The miracle was they expected him to stand and take a step or two with assistance in the next few days. He would have to be sitting and walking before he could go to a regular room. *That's a tall order for someone with his chest cracked open,* I thought. The girls came back in before he fell off again. I tried to touch him, but there were so many wires and tubes.

The nurse said, "It's okay, he will be back to sleep in just a split second."

The doctors messed with the IV lines once again and in just one blink of an eye John was back to sleep. John's complexion looked better. He was pink again. Any person without enough oxygen begins to look ashen, and that was how John had been looking lately. The girls took me to lunch, and we spent the rest of the day at the hotel just sleeping and watching television. Abbie looked through John's suitcase and found a package of brand new t-shirts.

"Could I paint on one of Dad's new shirts?" Abbie asked.

"Sure, that's a good idea," I told her. "What have you got in mind for the shirt?"

"Just wait and see, Momma," she said.

She went off into the sitting area of the suite and began on her project. This was Abbie's way of dealing with the stress and showing her dad how much she cares. She spent a great deal of time on it that evening. We looked up three scriptures she wanted to put around the image she had created. She hung it on a hanger and we all admired her work. John would love it. I stretched out and watched television for two seconds, the next thing I knew I awoke at five the next morning.

The girls were late sleepers, so I ordered up coffee and got ready for the day. If I got there early, I could catch the doctors, so I left a note and I was off. The hospital was only three minutes down Harry Hines Boulevard. I got to the ICU ward and the doctors had already been there, John's ventilator tube was out. He was propped up in bed and staring at the television screen. His head moved slightly when he saw me behind the glass door. The nurse motioned to go scrub up and come in to see him. I was so excited to see his baby blues bright and staring back at me. I smiled and told him I would do the talking. Tears ran down his face when I approached.

"You're doing great," I said. "The doctors are calling you a rock star."

I love you, Honey," John hoarsely whispered as tears ran down his face.

"I know your throat is sore so let me do the talking," I encouragingly said. "Just look what God has done. He has answered thousands of prayers. Everyone has texted and called me over the past three days, and they were lifting you up. I have kept them informed about your progress, so no worries. The doctors said you could get up and take steps tomorrow. They want you to get moving quickly."

John closed his eyes for a moment and I knew he would be asleep again shortly. His arms were strapped down to the bed so he would not pull at any of the wires or tubes. The doctors said the steroids might make him very emotional, so it had. He had been through the ringer, so to speak. Doctor Mullins approached as I came out into the hall. I was all smiles, and she knew that I was pleased with his progress. I gave her a hug as if she were my sister.

"We may have to shock him again," Dr. Mullins said.

"You mean he has gone into *afib* again?" I asked.

"Yes," she said, I have given John some medicine to see if it will work, and we should know in a short time."

I hadn't even noticed when I was in his room. I heard the monitor beeping but the nurse didn't seem alarmed. I went to the window and looked. Sure enough, his heartbeat was at one hundred forty-seven, jumping around to different numbers every two seconds. My mood tanked. He was napping, in and out, and I went back to the nurse's station to talk to the doctor one more time.

"John isn't sleeping in an induced coma now, so will he feel this or remember this?" I asked.

The doctor nodded her head and said, "Yes".

"Can't you put him back to sleep? I asked.

The doctor shook her head, no.
It upset me that he would have to go through this again.

"What happens if this keeps happening?" I asked.

"We will cross that bridge if this doesn't help. He is on a medicine that interferes with the heart rhythm meds, and we are trying to wean him off of it."

"So, when will you shock him again?"

"In a little while if the increased medicine doesn't work," Dr. Mullins said.

"Can I be close by again?" I asked.

"Yes, I will come out and let you know how it went," she reassured me.

Here I was all alone again, and this had to be done. I imagined all kinds of things if he was awake and getting shocked. I didn't want John to undergo anymore trauma, but this had to happen.

"Will you tell him what is going to happen?" I asked.

"Yes, and it will happen quickly," she said.

"Okay." I replied as I signed another form.

I watched the heart monitor the whole time bouncing up and down from one hundred forty four to one hundred sixty-nine. I didn't think that the meds were helping. I spoke to him when he was awake. He tried to say a word or two, but he was still hoarse from the ventilator tube. I asked him to close his eyes and rest. Thank God he did.

"I'll be here when you wake up."

"I'm seeing things," he whispered. "I see weird things. I'm seeing bugs and army guys coming out of the vents up there."

"It's the medicine, honey," I explained. "Your doctor said you will hallucinate on this high powered drug you have been on. It will take a day or two to get it out of your system."

"I can't close my eyes. I see mean evil people sometimes. It really scares me, Honey." John stated.

"Just keep your eyes open then," I told him, "and talk to me if you want to. God is right here, and your guardian angel is with us so there isn't anything to be frightened of."

"Okay," he said as he squeezed my hand.

I thought he was reassured that nothing was going to happen now. I knew he must be on some strong medicine. I grew up in the sixties when people took weird drugs and had hallucinations so this wasn't unfamiliar. John began to tell me about his father and that he saw him and thought he saw Jesus, too. He said he also saw his dad in our bedroom about a year ago. He swore it was real as rain. Who knows? God may send loved ones back to comfort us or still our fears. I don't know.

"I think it's just the drugs," John said.

"It may be," I told him, "but lots of people have had an experience like yours, and it was real to them."

I had one where I saw my great grandmother at the foot of my bed fifteen years after she died. I could describe her burial attire to a tee. I was a counselor in Bartlesville, Oklahoma at the time. She told me everything would be okay and to keep the faith. I don't know how she knew, but one of my students killed himself a month later. She was there to comfort me. I was a first year counselor, his death devastated me, and she let me know that God was there with me. When she appeared to me, I was so frightened that I called my mother at three o'clock in the morning to tell her what had just happened.

I was so grateful for His presence in our lives. I don't know how other people who don't know the love of Jesus make it in this world. John and I had a lot of things God wanted us to discover on this journey and the learning took place in our daily struggles. John had many things to discover in God's Word. I was astonished with what God had done in my life through the years. He allowed me to touch hundreds of lives through my profession. John and I were on God's teaching squad. Most of my life nearly all of my friends were on this squad as well. The friends that helped me the most are the ladies I served with at Chisholm Public Schools. The heart of this country can be found in its teachers. John's students sent cards and letters, and his staff at Shidler were of great comfort and support. We counted ourselves fortunate to know these outstanding people.

    I had a zillion text messages to answer. I sat and sent as many as I could, and then the doctor came into the room. I thought, *Oh boy she's going to tell him what is about to happen.* I looked over at John, and he had drifted back to sleep. As the doctors prepared, I slipped out of the room. It wasn't five minutes, and Doctor Mullins came out wearing a smile.

"It's done, and he's back in rhythm," Dr. Mullins said.

"Was he awake?" I asked quickly.

"He did wake up for a moment, but I don't think he will remember it," she said smiling.

"You're good, Doc." "Thank you so much," I said.

Well, once again, God was there protecting him from any more trauma. The girls arrived and the nurse let us all stay in the room. John began telling them about his hallucinating and seeing all kinds of things. They laughed and teased him about the bugs and army guys, and said they would like to have some of that medicine. He would hug his lung pillow when he got tickled and warned them he could not laugh. They were nuts! The nurse leaned towards me and said the laughter was good for him.

"Let's see if John can sit up on the side of the bed today," she said.

The nurse got a team of people into his ICU room and sat him up for ten minutes or so. John was so large they needed extra staff to help with the lifting. Then they carefully lowered him back down. With all the wires and tubing coming out of his lungs it was challenging. Tomorrow would be the big day, and John would stand and take some steps.

Four days after the surgery, the doctors expected John to stand and walk a few steps. The big guy did just that and more. He wanted to walk to the chair and sit awhile, and he did. When we put him back to bed, he was still hallucinating and would not close his eyes.

"Just rest awhile, I'll be right here." I said.

"I can't do it the bugs and army guys keep coming out of the vents. I think I saw the Hulk too," John said.

I patted him on the arm and said, "Talk to me, then. Your angel is standing right over there. I will stay until they give you medicine that makes you go back to sleep."

With the nurse standing so close, I didn't say anymore. I knew he was terrified. I pulled up a chair close enough to hold his hand. It was a simple joy just holding hands. I thanked God I still had his hand to hold. We watched television until dinner. He was expecting to get some food, but it was all soft or liquid. He drank everything on the tray and asked for more. This was a very good sign.

The girls came into his room in time to see him setting up in bed. No hugs or kisses but a lot of hand squeezing. Abbie was carrying a box with something inside.

"Dad, I have something for you," Abbie said. "No, it's not a steak. I made you a t-shirt that everyone that takes care of you can sign."

"That is cool!" John told her. "I love you."

It was beautiful. The t-shirt design had the hospital name around the neck written in a circular script. A big set of pink lungs with the blue Superman emblem in the center of the lungs were painted on the front of the shirt. The date of the transplant was large centered in the front and the scriptures circled the neck of the t-shirt, which were Matthew 7:7, Matthew 17:20, and Matthew 19:26.

We had looked them up together last night at the hotel. The nurses and the doctors loved it. Signatures from the medical staff and good wishes began showing up on it each day. The hospital gave each patient a pillow to hug when he or she had to cough. It was in the shape of a pair of lungs and dark pink. If you received a new heart, the pillow was in the shape of the heart. Family and friends signed the pillows, and it was an excellent keepsake. The t-shirt was a big hit and complimented the lung pillow perfectly.

Abbie was going home to Enid the next day. She had decided to move back home from Ponca City and had a lot to do. She promised her dad she would take care of grandma, the cattle, and the farm. She and Jordan, her roommate, were great friends and she was going to help as well. Katie returned to Moore and put Harry back in school. Lance made the trip to the farm and was holding the fort down until the girls were moved. We owed this young man a lot. John and I had terrific kids and they were all pulling together to help us. Not many people would quit their job and move home in an instant. Abbie was selfless and only thought of her parents in their time of need. My other support was leaving, but they promised me they would call every day.

Doctor Torres came by to see John, and it was so special. He was a very busy doctor. He had everything to do with us getting to Texas and saw that John had a shot at getting on a transplant list. He had a team of pulmonologists, and they would all have a turn at treating John before he would leave the hospital. Dr. Fernando Torres was the program director for the transplant team. The other doctors included Dr. Amit Banga, Dr. Srinivas Bollineni, Dr. Vaidehi Kasa, Dr. Manish Mohanka, and Dr. Jessica Mullins. At one time or another, John was under the care of every one of these great doctors. I have come to know each of them and I harbor an amazing respect for each of these caring professional doctors. There are no finer professionals in this country than the ones I have just mentioned. Dr. Torres stopped by and bragged on John's amazing progress. He looked at the incision and the tubes and it all looked good. In a few days, John would be moved to a regular hospital room. John showed him the t-shirt and asked him to sign it. He was happy to do it.

CHAPTER SEVEN
"The Arrival"

By late morning on Friday, our daughters were heading back to Oklahoma. Katie had to return to work at the beauty school and Harry had to return to pre-k.

Abbie and Jordan had to give notice at work and pack up their house within a few weeks. Lance would cover all the bases at the farm until the girls could be moved. The biggest chores were mowing five acres and distributing hay and cubes for the cattle. The grass was coming in and feeding would be finished soon. The information we had been given for the length of our time here in Dallas was six months to one year depending on John's progress. Carrie, Lance's wife, took care of any needs here while we were in Dallas while her husband would go to

Oklahoma. I had been told not to worry about anything at home. God provided everyone and everything. I would not live long enough to pay it all forward; we were so blessed. I had to find an apartment or a cheaper hotel. It was becoming too expensive to keep staying at the Holiday Inn. Katie found the David Nicklas Foundation that very morning. A foundation that provided apartments for transplant candidates or patients and their families. Katie called and the last apartment became available that day. She was on the phone with them.

Katie promptly said, "We want it! I will have my mom over this afternoon to sign the papers."

The apartment complex was the Landings of Carrier Parkway. *That's funny we live on Carrier Road,* I thought. The main office area had a spacious clubroom with a bar and a computer room that was available to transplant patients. They had an exercise room with all the equipment and a lovely swimming pool. The manager showed us the one bedroom apartment, equipped with dishes, linens, washer/dryer, and television. It had a queen bed and the restroom off the bedroom. The living and kitchen area were all one room with a small utility room for the washer and dryer. It was ready to move into right then and there.

This unit was sponsored by a big corporate bank. The name of the sponsor was on a plaque above the front outer door. The foundation was formed when the builder of the complex received a heart from a young man named David Nicklas. He was tragically killed and was an organ donor. His sister, Rebecca, is the Director of Operations for the foundation. The story was so wonderfully beautiful. There was a plaque and story posted in the front lobby of the club house. Every person who had ever stayed there waiting or recovering from a transplant had his or her picture on the wall of fame. As I walked by the pictures I thought, *someday John will have his picture up there.*

The girls had to shove off for Oklahoma, but wanted to see where I would reside while in Dallas. With kisses and hugs, they promised to call when they arrived, and they were gone. Emptiness loomed after the departure. I had suitcases to unpack and my niece, Carrie, helped me get the television going. I was set. I only had to pay utilities and cable. This was so unbelievable, for it was expensive living in the Dallas area. I was twenty minutes away from downtown Dallas and Clements University Hospital. This would be my home for the next six months to a year.

The traffic was an episode in a horror story. Anyone who is not a Christian should not take I-30 on a weekday morning headed east to Dallas or west to Ft. Worth. From six o'clock until nine o'clock in the morning traffic zoomed by on George W. Bush Presidential Toll Way near my apartment. The exit ramps to Dallas or Ft. Worth were a mile down this highway. Thousands of cars bumper to bumper sped by. I had not experienced traffic as one of my familiar sounds for the past ten years. We lived on an isolated dirt road. Not many cars or trucks flew by our house at six in the morning. I drove to work six miles and had only one stop sign on the way. The traffic sounds in Dallas became my alarm clock. I did not even think of getting out on that road until after nine. My life flashed before my eyes, as raging and angry people rushed to work.

Well, God had taken care of everything right down to where I would lay my head at night. I didn't know how long we would be here, but this gated community was beautiful, and I felt safe in the big city. I hadn't lived in an apartment since I was single. It was an adjustment. I could hear people upstairs, which made for a sleepless first night. I missed having my daughters around me. They were more support than they would ever know. I owed them so much. I am ever so proud of them. They had bloomed into beautiful young women, and they stepped up to one of life's challenges and showed their parents what they were made of. I thanked God for such children. Alone I missed the constant revelations of city life when they were in Dallas like the traffic, Six Flags, Ripley's Believe It or Not, the Aquarium, and so many other things that my Oklahoma country girls had not experienced. I mostly missed their laughter and looked forward to a call every now and then. I was lonely already, and it had only been two days without them.

 I quickly fell into a routine each morning. Up and out the door to the hospital by nine o'clock. This particular morning I found John walking down the hall with two nurses following him. He had a walker to help him keep his balance. This was something new getting him out of the room. He had on a surgical mask, some gloves, and a hospital gown with pajama pants underneath. On his size fifteens, he was wearing white socks. He acted as if he was tooling down a lazy river on a Sunday morning.

"Well, look at you, Mr. Smarty Pants," I teased him.

"Hey, the doctors told me I'm going to a regular room today."

The nurses nodded their heads and agreed that he was getting out of ICU today.

"Oh, you are kidding me," I said.

We walked to his room, and I packed up his two pair of pajama bottoms in his overnight bag. Before long, a nurse and two other orderlies with a wheel chair came into move him to the tenth floor. John refused the wheel chair.

"I want to walk to the elevator," John said.

As he made it to the elevator, Liz and Marty poked their heads out of the waiting room and noticed John.

"Take care of that big drink of water," Liz said.

John wheeled around, moved towards her, and gave her a big hug.

"I'm praying for Wendell," he told her. "Tana has kept me informed about him."

I had never seen or met Wendell, but I knew he was a rounder by the conversations Liz and I had had over the last week. Wendell was an ornery, independent fellow. I hoped I would get to meet him someday. It is so strange how one can automatically have a connection with those who are going through the same valley. I'd become attached to her and prayed for her husband each night. I went looking for her each day after first seeing John. I was going to miss my friend even though were would just be up on floor ten. I exchanged telephone numbers in case we missed each other at the hospital.

John turned and headed to the elevator with all the nurses following behind him. One nurse kept the wheel chair behind him in case he became too tired to continue walking. We all got on the elevator and rode up to the tenth floor.

"Do you want to ride to your new room?" the nurse asked.

"No, I'm going to walk," John proudly said.

The room was very spacious and had a long couch that made out into a bed. Just in case I needed to stay with John there was a place for me. Solid glass windows from top to bottom were overlooking downtown Dallas. It had a large flat-screened television attached to the wall, a big easy chair placed in the corner by the patient's bed, and a big bathroom with shower and sink set off to the opposite corner of the room. A solid wall of windows provided the view of downtown Dallas. You could see the high-rise towers and planes from Love Field fly by the window. It was a beautiful room. Room number 1011 was John's new home for a while. Now just seven days later after his surgery, he was in a regular hospital room. Seven days, God's fingerprint was evident once again. His mighty hand had been on everything so far on our journey. I was astonished with the reminders that *"God's got this."*

The physical therapy team was in his room a lot. They worked him out good. John's doses of steroids wreaked havoc on his blood sugar. It forced him to take insulin four times a day. He would be a diabetic for the rest of his life. He also had to watch his diet because of potential weight gain. The nurses began showing us how to test and administer insulin in his thigh or on the back of his arm.

This would become a lifetime routine because of the steroids that were required to fight rejection of the lungs. The steroids also had an adverse effect on John emotionally, causing moodiness and anxiety. His hands shook, and it was difficult for him to remaster many fine motor skills efficiently. The number of medicines he was taking grew to four pages in length. We were issued a book with the medications, alongside forms for recording blood pressure, temperature, heart rate, blood sugar levels, and a spirometer to measure his lungs' performance. The pharmacist came up to his room to teach us about each medication. John had to fill his weekly medicine container. This was a tedious task with him shaking so badly.

"Watch John place all of his meds into the small squares for the four times a day he will take medicine," the pharmacists told me.

This took some time with all the pill bottles to go through. The medicine had to be taken on time to prevent any rejection symptoms. I was to use a mask and gloves when preparing his food or helping with the medicines. My thoughts swirled. I kept saying to myself, we can do this. It will not overwhelm us, and it will become routine. They were preparing to kick us out of the nest.

"John will get to go to your apartment in a few days," the nurse said.

Then I would be responsible for all his medical needs. I was scared straight. I was studying, trying to learn all I could from the medical team. The caregiver keeps them on schedule; the twist was that they added antibiotics to the mix, and I was going to administer those through a picline. They had surgically placed this line into John's right arm. The line went to portals that a syringe would hook into with caps to cover them. They had to be kept clean. I was to give antibiotics and heparin through the lines. The doctor came by, and she said John was about ready to go home; he was progressing so well.

"Dr. Mullins, this new technology will be a success judging by John's amazing progress, right?" I asked.

"Did you see the lungs in the bell jar?" I asked her.

"Oh, yeah," she said. "Do you want to see a picture of the lungs that are in John right now?" Dr. Mullins asked.

I nodded, and she got her smart phone out, found her pictures, handed me the phone, and showed me. I had never seen a set of lungs except on an x-ray. These were pink and inflated. I wondered who the person was that gave them to John. I just stared at the lungs. How in the world did they make this all work?

"How many people have had lungs off this ex-vivo technology?" I asked her.

"Your husband is the very first in Texas to receive lungs from this technology," she said.

I looked at her in amazement and said, "You mean no one else has done this?"

"No, not in Texas," she replied.

"So they didn't know if this would work or not?" I asked.

"Yes, there have been some done at other clinical sites participating in the trial in the United States," she said, but "John is our rock star in Texas."

God had chosen the lungs from someone that were just the right size, blood type, tissue type, and all the other markers necessary for a match to John. God had given the doctors this new technology to restore the lungs then provided the first opportunity to John for this procedure that ultimately was to be used to save lives in the future. How much grace was in this act from our loving God? I was speechless when I became aware of what had really taken place. Nothing was impossible for God. John was living His miracle.

According to Doctor Mullins John was exceeding all expectations. I left the hospital knowing I needed to get some rest because my work was about to begin. I felt scared, so I spoke to God, as I slipped off to sleep.

I had the apartment ready for John. I couldn't believe it had been thirteen days since the transplant. When I got to John's room, a big nurse with a gruff voice had just entered the room.

"Hi, my name is Maryann," she said, "They call me the hog butcher."

John and I just looked at each other. She was there to remove the tubes out of both sides of his chest. She rolled John on his side like she was rolling a biscuit.

"Take a big breath," she said.

Before John or I knew it, the tube was out.

Maryann said, "One more and we're finished here."

It happened so fast there wasn't time for anticipating any pain. She placed a bandage on the holes, and she was gone. She did take time to sign John's shirt. She wrote: "Maryann, The hog butcher." She was proud of her title.

John had one more test and then we were going to be released from the hospital that afternoon. The swallow test was given, so he could eat solid food after he left the hospital. His esophagus had been moved during the surgery and had some swelling, so they were concerned about it functioning properly. The doctors took pictures of him swallowing while eating different things to determine whether or not he could eat solid food. He came back to the room from this test; he'd failed it. The nurse told us he would have to puree all his food for the next week until the next test. I knew that eating baby food for that long wasn't going to go over with John.

The doctor entered and announced John would not go home today. The delay was due to concern with the swallowing. I was relieved for now, and I had time to purchase the puree machine that night at Walmart. He was going to kill me forcing him eat this baby food. I knew this would be a dangerous week for the hired help. I had plenty of experience with this, and you did not withhold food from Big John. Cranky wasn't an adequate adjective for our first day.

The cook, nurse, counselor, chauffeur, secretary, and linen maid woke up and immediately called John at the hospital.

"Good Morning, Puss," I said. "I will be there soon to break you out."

He was in good spirits. I was so very nervous about him coming to the apartment. I had been given so much responsibility. I felt so very alone. I prayed for strength and for the help of God to face all the changes that had and would occur in our lives. I headed for downtown Dallas to get my John.

When I entered the room the doctor had not been by yet, John was anxious to get out of there. He had been driving the nurses crazy with all the walking he would do. Sometimes they couldn't find him when it was time for his medications because he was out walking the halls.

I sat down and glanced at my phone the date was April eighteenth. Exactly seven days in a regular hospital room. Another seven, God's fingerprint, had developed.

John could not drive for at least four months post-surgery, so I drove Mr. Daisy everywhere. He had two carts full of meds and personal belongings to load in the truck. I took pictures of him coming out of the hospital. What a milestone. He was on Facebook and texting all the way to Grand Prairie, Texas, which is a suburb of Dallas. The commute was less than twenty minutes if there wasn't any traffic. He called the girls first and all our friends and family back home. FaceTime is a wonderful invention for all the grandparents in the world. Oh, how we missed seeing Harry the past few weeks. They grow so fast! Seeing them every day was a blessing. Harry was four years old and beginning kindergarten. We didn't want to miss any of it. As I drove, I thought about the impossible that had just happened and the reality that we were going to our apartment. The relief of knowing he was going to be around to watch his grandson grow up and spend additional time with his family warmed my heart. I wanted to hug everyone who had supported us and prayed for John's recovery.

    The next morning I had to speed down I-30 East to get John back to the emergency room at Clements University Hospital. He had a terrible night and something wasn't right so we returned to the hospital. I had called our transplant coordinator, David, who'd said to get back to the hospital right away. Sure enough, the doctors checked him back into the hospital. John had become dehydrated and his medications weren't right.

John spent another four days in the hospital on the tenth floor. The nurses smiled at him saying to John, "What are you doing back here?" They were all so kind and took excellent care of him. John felt better being at the hospital. Even I had to admit, I felt better too. I was not at all sure I could care for him until he was a little better. He was on a blood thinner, had an incision that had not healed, his sternum was wired together, a picline hung off his right arm, and he had four holes on both sides of his chest. He shook because of the steroids and had to have a walker for his balance. I was relieved he was under the nurses' care once again. I slept better while he was at the hospital. I was not anxious to kill him under my care. The pressure was off me. I was not very good nursing material. He was stable and resting, and I was glad to be back.

I went to the cafeteria and on the way back I got off on the ninth floor. Liz was in the waiting room with some other people around her. I approached her, and she left the group and hugged me. We just lost Wendell. Tears welled up as I was hugging her; she was already crying. I was crushed for her. She and Marty had hoped for a miracle just like the one that John had received. It was not to be.

I told her I would call her and keep in contact. I felt as if she were a relative. We had an instant connection and prayed with each other during this journey. She had suffered such a loss. This was the moment when people ask why one lived and the other died. I wrote to her after the funeral and hoped all of her children and grandchildren surrounded her. I continued to pray for her and still do to this day. She called me on the phone after she received a Christmas card, and I assured her I would come to see her when John was more independent.

After four days, John was much better, and they sent us back to the apartment. We began clinical two days later. We got into the routine of getting up at five thirty or six in the morning two days a week. Fought the traffic and then on to the lab for blood tests and x-rays, then up to the sixth floor to see David and the doctors. We'd enter check in and the waiting rooms would usually be full of other transplant recipients who were in a surgical masks and gloves going through the same procedures. Some of them had this routine down; you could tell they had been doing this for a long time. We saw our go to guy, David, each time, and he'd take so much time and care with John. He was our go to guy twenty-four hours a day seven days a week. He had been doing this for some time and was good at his job. He knew what to say and when to ask the right questions. He was an upbeat nurse with tons of knowledge and the doctors trusted him. So many things could have gone wrong, and David seemed to catch them all right in time, so we could change course. I called David for all questions and all medical inconsistencies. I became very attached to him. He always consulted with me on John's progress. All the medical staff knew John; his Superman status had spread to the clinic as well. They all knew he was the UT Southwestern success story. We continued this schedule for a month, and then twice a month, and finally, down to just once a month. We were told we'd be doing this for the rest of John's life.

During the month of June, we left the apartment to see some of the local sights. We drove around the Dallas Fort Worth area and visited antique shops and a few paint galleries. We had apartment fever and made any excuse to go to Wal-Mart or Sam's Club.

We would call the farm and see what was going on and how everyone was doing. One weekend the tribe had met there to do some work. They were all there cooking out that evening. Curiously, I asked what was for dinner. They all yelled at the same time, steaks. You could hear them all laughing. We were down in Texas, and they were enjoying our homegrown beef. John and I just looked at each other and knew that they wiped out our freezer. We had a calf butchered, and they were eating all our steaks. Oh well, the price you pay for the unhired help. Abbie and Jordan were coming at the end of the month to spend the weekend with us. It was Abbie's twenty-fifth birthday, and we were going to treat her to the Aquarium and a fancy dinner out. We were homesick; we missed our family and friends. John and I had cabin fever. John was tired of me, and I was tired of looking at his mug twenty-four seven, but I still loved him!

The University of Texas Southwestern was one of sixteen locations in the United States participating in the ex-vivo technology trials. This technology was new and was currently used in Japan and Canada. These trials were necessary for FDA approval in this country.

The medical team and doctors had kept the media away from us all this time. It was now June, and they felt John could finally tell his story. The University would get the media coverage and exposure for the only transplant program in the state of Texas participating in the national trials using this technology. John was the first man in Texas to receive lungs from the bell jar, a nickname for the ex-vivo technology. The lungs in John's body would have been thrown away if not for this technology. What was remarkable was how they refurbished the lungs after they harvested them. They left them in the bell jar for hours until the doctors believed they were viable for transplantation.

The public relations representative, Cathy Frisinger, for UT Southwestern came by to visit with John and wrote his story for the university medical newspaper called Center Times. Cathy did all the coordinating with the television stations and the newspapers in Dallas and around the country. Our hometown newspaper picked it up quickly and friends called to tell us that John made the front page of the Enid News and Eagle. Many tiny newspapers picked up the story, but we never received copies of their releases. The Dallas Morning News published John's story in the Arts and Life section of the newspaper. Hannah Fleace wrote the story "Breathing on His Own". She portrayed us as we really were. Grateful for what this procedure had provided us. It was additional time on this earth with family and friends, and it is priceless.

The *Channel 11 News* station in Dallas was the first to film John. We got permission for them to come to the clubhouse of the Landings of Carrier Parkway for the shoot and interview. John always tried to tell his story honestly and give some kind words about the Nicklas Foundation furnishing an apartment for us. He was very humble and wanted to do anything to pay it forward so that others could take advantage of this technology. There were so many waiting and not enough lungs available. People waiting for lungs died at their apartments. Every time we heard sirens enter the complex we prayed.

John and I both became organ donors and encouraged as many people as we could to become organ donors too. It is easy to do and everyone should consider it. In Oklahoma, you can indicate that you are a donor when applying for a driver's license and a heart is added to signify this decision.

On the last day of June, the doctors gave us permission to make a short visit home during the Fourth of July holiday. We were beside ourselves, called the kids, and told them we'd get to come home for a short visit. July 2016 was the seventh month and July 4th marked exactly three months since John had received the transplant. This marked the seventh seven recorded on our journey.

What a difference a year makes. God had brought John and me full circle. He now walked two miles in the apartment complex parking lot each evening. He was feeling so good, and his blood sugar was somewhat under control. Independence Day had a new meaning this year. Coming home to the farm and having the kids there with us was so special.

It was strange having been gone for months. The comfort of my own bed and easy chair was indescribable. Clothes I had forgotten about until I opened the closet door helped me appreciate the warmth of coming home. My favorite coffee cup and having coffee on the screened in porch is how we savored life's moments. Everything was still green except the harvested wheat fields. I was draped with gratefulness. I could not thank God in heaven enough for His miracle. John and I were swept with euphoria; I knew I had lived out His miracle with my husband. I knew the love that others had for our family because of the prayers sent to our Father. I was anxious to discover the plan God had for John and me to pay it forward. Any family that has been tested knows that God is Love; and there is no way to love Him more than He loves you. If a person doesn't know this love, then they are missing the reason we were created.

    I slept the entire night through and felt great peace the first night home. The holiday was different but lovely. We missed the tribe and all the fireworks. With the cookout and the family games postponed, but we looked forward to next year. Our holiday went by too quickly. We had to return to Dallas and did not know when we would have our next homecoming.

John's high school friends set up a go fund me account to help with the medical expenses. Their concern for John and all the many others who contributed to this fund will hopefully know the gratitude we have for this kindness. This helped us tremendously and took the financial pressure off while John was recovering from surgery. We received so many contributions that I cannot mention them all, but we would like to thank you. We are overwhelmed at the task of paying this forward and pray God will show us a way.

The month of August was hot in big D, and we were stuck in the apartment most of the time. We fell back into our routine of going to clinical and seeing the doctors. They took John off Rythmol, which was the medicine he was taking to regulate his heart rhythm. This was the medicine Dr. Mullins put him on after transplant when he was experiencing *afib*. John had a super checkup, and the doctor told us we could go home permanently to Enid, and return once a month for appointments starting in September. We looked at each other with big smiles of amazement. The doctor had just unlocked the handcuffs. We were going home for good. We would visit Dallas and not have to live there anymore.

    I was totally exhausted and was more than ready to get home to family and friends. I needed some support, but we still needed to be careful and adhere to the rules. We rushed back to the apartment and decided to pack and leave the next day. We decided to keep the apartment for one more month in case of an emergency. We would come back, clean, and shut off utilities in September. We had a pickup full of things, but we had lots of help when we pulled into the driveway to unload.

We quickly fell into a routine with meals, meds, and the constant cleaning. We had family dinners each night. Everyone took a night so five nights a week the cook was different. This helped me out on meal planning. Abbie, Jordan, and Grandma took their turn. John took a night of cooking as well. John ate heartily because of the steroids, so we planned a lot of salads, veggies, and hid the sweet things in the pantry. The steroids could also make John moody or aggressive but they rarely did so.

We were getting settled back in at home when John suddenly slipped back into *afib*. He was sitting in his easy chair, and his heart was racing. He had a meter that measured the rate, and it was one hundred fifty or better and continually jumping around. This was what happened in the hospital after the transplant. We had to get to the hospital. I rushed him to Integris Bass Hospital in Enid where he stabilized. The doctors called UT Southwestern giving John's vitals and information to the transplant coordinator. We headed to Dallas that very evening and checked John in the hospital through the ER.

I was glad we had the apartment. They sent him back to the cardiac doctors; the Rythmol was back in his regiment of medicines for life. Every time we had an emergency, it took a little more out of me. This was the third trip back to the hospital since the surgery. Exhaustion and mental anguish had taken a toll on me. Two days later, we returned to the farm and started living every moment. We had to find the new normal with the regiment of medicine, meals, exercise, and sanitary regulations to prevent anyone from becoming ill.

As we settled into our new normal, I felt the plane's tires touch down on the asphalt, and I could hear the engines reversing to slow the momentum of the airplane. We had gradually slowed and were pulling into the terminal when the captain came on the intercom and said, "Thank you for traveling with God's Airlines and we hope you will remember us when you travel again."

EPILOGUE

Our grandson was in kindergarten in Enid and very happy this year. He played soccer for the first time this year. The shorts, jersey, and special socks with shin guards in them, and his spiked shoes were a kill. He dressed the part. We went to all his matches. The little players kept us in stitches. They would run from one end to the other. Not many goals were scored, but the geese flew both ways.

Sometimes I would glance over at John and see he was taking it all in as well. The joy of him watching his grandson and encouraging him to go get the ball was priceless. Harry would become tired from all the running and then just squat down and rest awhile. The game would just go on without him. When the quarter was over, they would change and let the others have a go at it. During one of these changes, I called Harry over for his drink and he chugged it down.

"Granny, I don't like getting hot," he said.

Right then I knew our grandson would not be a professional athlete. Harry began taking vacuums apart at the age of three to see how they worked. He is still doing that as of today. He has more knowledge of the different brands of vacuums than anyone I know. A Wal-Mart trip always includes a stroll down the vacuum isle to see if there are any new models. Nerd was the term we gave the smart kids in school that loved math and had a big curiosity about how things worked. I'm blessed to have such a wonderful nerd. The last nut on this bolt was when Harry came to me one day and said.

"Granny, I want some of those pens that stick to you."

Well. I thought a minute and said, "You want the pens that fit into a pocket and have a little bar that attaches to your pocket?"

"Yes!" he said so excitedly.

I found some, and he clipped them to his shirt and ran off happy as could be. We love having our grandson close.

Thanksgiving week Harry invited his Grandfather to eat at this year's kindergarten feast. Usually, the week before the actual holiday Chisholm Elementary has turkey and dressing and all the fixings' at school. The kids give thanks and let God know what they are thankful for this year. They wear pilgrim hats and Indian headdresses full of feathers, all made from construction paper, to the feast. John was grateful to be there for this special event. Harry loved being a Chisholm Longhorn, and events like this one, were only one of many that make life at this school so special. Things were not back to normal. We didn't know what that was now. There is only today and each day was a blessing for which I am truly grateful.

The Herzig family celebrated Christmas with only immediate family members this past year. I liked that because we often tried to cram too much and too many into this holiday. Harry and I decorated the tree and sang "Santa Claus Is Coming to Town." We set up Santa's Christmas band that played songs using bells. This band kept him entertained. He watched them forever so long. It never became tiresome for Harry and he turned them on each day before Christmas.

Harry proudly let all of us know that he was finished decorating and to come and look. A few more ornaments were decked on the right side of the tree, but it was beautiful. In a few days, packages began arriving. Fed Ex came to the farm every day with packages. Lots and lots of packages arrived for Harry and Katie. A special friend was sending Katie and Harry a package each day before

Christmas to put under the tree. Harry would come home from school to see what was new each day. He picked the packages up and would give them a good shake.

"What's in there?" I would ask.

"I don't know," he replied grinning.

I knew Katie's friend in California was sending all these gifts to the farm. She had mentioned Adam was coming to Oklahoma for Christmas. His family lived in Oklahoma City, so he would be here for the holidays. I commented on all the packages under the tree.

"Adam wanted us to have a special Christmas this year," Katie cheerfully said.

"This must be a serious friendship," I said with a smile.

I left it at that and refrained from becoming a nosy mother. As more gifts arrived, Harry's eyes lit up. What a nice young man, I thought. Adam was a real writer and pursuing a career in the film industry. He came to the farm to visit us for the day before

Christmas and it was a lovely day. We all exchanged gifts and got to know each other. To Adam I am truly thankful for his help in recording John's story and the kindness he has shown to my daughter and grandson.

Just a few days prior to Christmas, Channel 9 News in Oklahoma City aired John's story. The reporter and camera crew had come up to the farm in October for the interview. It was very touching and emotional when John told his story. The reporter and crew also went to UT Southwestern, talked to Dr. Torres, and viewed the ex-vivo machine. The news station tied it all together and made a special short story that hit home for the Christmas season. Many friends and relatives after the broadcast called and commented on the emotional events we had endured, and how special this Christmas must be for the Herzig Family. It was indeed!

My nephew, Lance, called from time to time and prayed with me for the strength to continue as John's number one. I was tired, anxious, and mentally overtaxed. I was lost in all the stress, and it was hard to find time for just me. That sounded selfish, but I had been under stress for twenty-one months of nonstop doctor appointments, clinical appointments, medicines, meals, and all his needs that I needed to take care of. For most of it, I had no relief because we were in Texas. I don't think I could have come this far without the prayer and love of friends and family.

When the music stopped, I couldn't find myself. I tried to take time with my friends and get away, but it was not enough and much too late. I found no interest in the things I used to enjoy. I robotically performed the maid and cooking duties. I systematically cleaned the bathroom and kitchen, so John would not get sick. I constantly did things so John would not get sick. It never stopped. I could never relax. The reality of the situation was my needs had stopped. Life was forever changed to this type of activity for me in my mind. It was not healthy. I knew things had to change for me in order to find me again. If John did not follow protocols like wearing a mask and all the other rules, I felt obliged to remind him. I was a nag, and he would become angry. I was basically the germ police.

I believed I was depressed and grieving for the life we once had which was now so different. Things we thought we'd do together, we now knew would probably never happen. John was doing well, but I realized he could not keep this farm going. I was stuck with a lot of different fears. One big fear was not taking all the precautions and something awful happening to John. I was the proverbial fireman always at the firehouse and waiting for the alarm to go off. I could not cope with daily things and got so upset. I had definitely lost touch with me. I read my Bible every day and spent my time in prayer, but I wasn't getting any better.

"I need a big hug, God," I pleaded as I talked to Him.

My armor was a little dented. We had been in the fight for John's life. I sat on the floor to polish it and tried to straighten out the dents and damage by studying and reading the powerful Word of God. I searched for a new purpose that He had in store for me. I was more than weary. Jesus said, "Come unto me all you who are weary and heavy laden, and I will give you rest." (Matthew 11:28) *KJV*. So this was where I went to bury myself in the Word each morning. The grieving was for the death of our old lives together, and I worried about all the things John must do to keep on living.

During the winter months, John and I had been so isolated and that only added to my depression. With so many rules about avoiding crowds during the cold and flu season, we were limited from doing a lot of activities in the winter months for John's safety. Anyone living in our house had to have the flu shot. The statistics reveal after one year the survival rates of lung recipients was seventy-eight percent. After three years, the life expectancy fell to fifty-eight percent. Life expectancy dropped lower with each passing year. The lungs are the most difficult organs, because they are constantly exposed to the outside world with all its germs.

    I have been working through my grief and depression with the help of friends and a professional. I venture out more and volunteered three hours a week at Harry's school. I play with my grandson more, and let the housework go. I realized I couldn't be responsible for all that happens to John. I can only live in each moment and love him with all my heart. It is a simple concept that God has told us to do for over two thousand years. The transplant experience from beginning to present for me has been the most traumatic, emotional, and spiritual journey I've experienced to date.

Life's lesson has been learning to trust and obey my Father. My faith in Him has intensified through this experience. I feel closer to my creator and know that He is always beside me. I have changed and so has John; our entire family's salvation is secure. God wants us to contribute to building His kingdom through our testimony to others. The things we thought were important before have little importance now. Showing and seeking others to share in the love of Jesus will be our privilege for the rest of our journey. We all will surely reach our appointed time to die, but God has assigned John's flight for another time.

A year ago, John was given the gift of life. We have reached out to the family of the donor through a letter with hopes that they will want to meet John one day. We wanted the opportunity to tell the donor family in person what their gift has done for him. This process was delicate and was handled through the University of Texas Southwestern to preserve and to respect the privacy of each family.

GOD'S FINGERPRINT

7th Month	John was diagnosed July 2015
7 Months	John worked to get on a list.
	September 4, 2015-March 29th 2016
7 Days	John was on the list March 29th 2016
	Notified of Transplant April 4th 2016
7 Hours	Entered Surgery 11:00 a.m.
	Completed Surgery 6:00 p.m.
7 Days	Length of ICU stay. April 5-11th, 2016
7 Days	Length of stay Regular Hospital Room
	April 12-18th 2016
7th Month	Homecoming July 4th 2016

God's presence was felt the entire journey. Seven sevens had occurred and John was totally restored. The number seven is the most significant number in the Bible. Seven signifies perfection and completeness, which is exemplified throughout the Bible. Some of God's examples of using the number seven are: Seven days for creation thus the number of days in a week, seven days of festivals and wedding celebrations, we are to forgive seven times seventy, and the year of Jubilee comes after seven times seven or every forty-nine years.

I first noticed the pattern of sevens when I glanced at the date the morning of John's surgery while I was sitting in the waiting room. He had been on the transplant list for seven days when he received lungs. I had recorded dates and events in my Bible as we went along this journey, and as I reviewed them, I noticed several instances where sevens turned up in hours, days, and months, during the year. Our journey began in the seventh month of 2015, and John's homecoming occurred the seventh month of 2016. John's seven sevens resulted in his personal Jubilee. We thank the Creator for his grace and mercy.

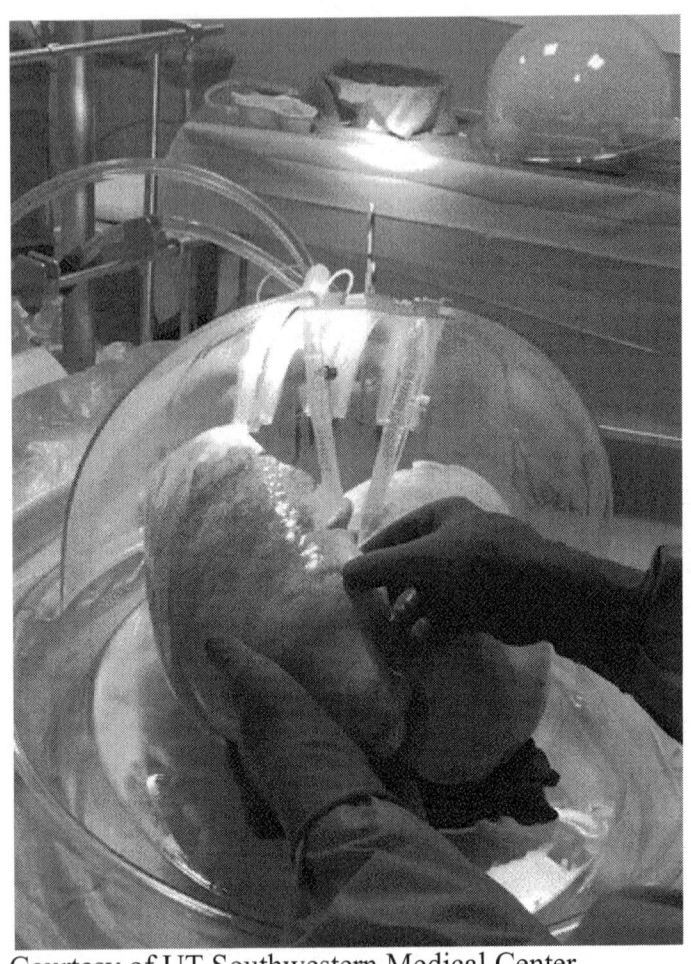

Courtesy of UT Southwestern Medical Center

Made in the USA
San Bernardino, CA
17 December 2017